£4.99

CM0074191Z

Exodus

An Agenda for Jewish-Christian Dialogue

By the same author

A Dictionary of Judaism and Christianity
Holocaust Theology
Issues in Contemporary Judaism
Jewish Petitionary Prayer: A Theological Exploration
On Earth as it is in Heaven: Jews, Christians and
    Liberation Theology
Rabbinic Perspectives on the New Testament
The Crucified Jew: Twenty Centuries of Christian
    Anti-Semitism
The Jewish Heritage
The Jews of Canterbury
The Blackwell Dictionary of Judaica
Israel: The History of an Idea

As editor

Many Mansions: Interfaith and Religious Intolerance
A Traditional Quest: Essays in Honour of Louis Jacobs
Problems in Contemporary Jewish Theology
Exploring Reality
Islam in a World of Diverse Faiths
Religion in Public Life
The Canterbury Papers: Essays on Religion and Society
The Salman Rushdie Controversy in Interreligious
    Perspective
The Sayings of Moses
Tradition and Unity: Sermons Published in Honour of
    Robert Runcie
Using the Bible Today: Contemporary Interpretations
    of Scripture
World Religions and Human Liberation

EXODUS

*An Agenda for
Jewish-Christian Dialogue*

Dan Cohn-Sherbok

Bellew Publishing
London

First published in Great Britain in 1992 by
Bellew Publishing Company Limited
Nightingale Centre
8 Balham Hill
London SW12 9EA

ISBN 1 85725 039 7

Phototypeset by Intype, London
Printed and bound in Great Britain by
Billings & Sons Ltd

Acknowledgements

I would like to thank Justine Clements of
Rutherford College Secretarial Office for
typing the manuscript and Susanna Burt of
Bellew for her help.

For Maria and Ian

Contents

This is the bread of affliction that our fathers
ate in the land of Egypt. All who hunger,
let them come and eat: all who are in need,
let them come and celebrate the Passover.
Now we are here – next year we shall be
free.

Passover Haggadah

Introduction: From Holocaust to Renewal

A little before seven, there was an announcement: 'The first train will arrive in ten minutes!' A few minutes later a train arrived from Lemberg: forty-five carriages with more than six thousand people . . . A loudspeaker gave instructions: 'Strip, even artificial limbs and glasses. Hand all money and valuables in at the "valuables" window' . . . Stark naked men, women, children and cripples passed by . . . SS men pushed the men into chambers . . . Seven to eight hundred people in ninety-three square metres. The doors closed . . . Twenty-five minutes passed. You could see through the windows that many were already dead, for an electric light illuminated the interior of the room . . . All were dead after thirty-two minutes . . . The people were still standing like columns of stone, with no room to fall or lean. Even in death you could tell the families, all holding hands . . .

Only fifty years ago millions of Jews lost their lives in such a fashion – yet the people survived the Nazi onslaught. And once Hitler had been defeated, the Jewish community affirmed its commitment to Jewish survival through the establishment of a homeland in Palestine. Having emerged from the prospect of annihilation, the Jewish people in the latter half of this century have flourished in Israel and elsewhere.

None the less the nightmare of the Holocaust continues to haunt Jewry: it has deepened the Jewish determination to defend the State of Israel and ensure that Jews everywhere are protected from anti-Semitic attack. Further, the murder of millions of Jews at the hands of the Nazis has

1

persuaded many Jews that Jewish self-interest must prevail over all other concerns. For most Jews today, what is required is the commitment to the continuation of Judaism and the Jewish nation.

Such an attitude has been most eloquently expressed by the Jewish theologian Emil Fackenheim, who insists that it is a sacred duty to respond to the Holocaust. The intention of the Nazis was to eliminate all Jews; no survivor was to be left to tell the story of what horrors took place. However, Fackenheim insists that in the death camps the Voice of God was heard. Out of the ashes of the crematoria God issued a further command. This 614th commandment (added to the 613 prescriptions contained in the Torah) is directed to the post-Holocaust Jewish community. According to Fackenheim:

> Jews are forbidden to hand Hitler posthumous victories. They are commanded to survive as Jews, lest the Jewish people perish. They are commanded to remember the victims of Auschwitz lest their memory perish. They are forbidden to despair of man and his world, and to escape into either cynicism or other worldliness, lest they co-operate in delivering the world over to the forces of Auschwitz. Finally, they are forbidden to despair of the God of Israel, lest Judaism perish . . . A Jew may not respond to Hitler's attempt to destroy Judaism by himself co-operating in its destruction. In ancient times, the unthinkable Jewish sin was idolatry. Today it is to respond by doing his work. (Fackenheim, 1970, 81)

In this theological formulation Fackenheim has given voice to a universal sentiment expressed by contemporary Jewry: Never Again! In a post-Holocaust world, the quest for Jewish survival has understandably eclipsed all other matters. However, such a focus of Jewish life has turned Jewry inwards – in its determination to endure at all costs, the universalism of biblical and rabbinic Judaism has been suppressed. More specifically, the Jewish preoccupation with survival has tended to blind the Jewish people to the needs of those non-Jews who are presently undergoing hardship similar to that which the Jewish people endured through the centuries. In this respect contemporary Jewry has lost sight of the prophetic vision of the Jewish people as a light to the nations.

How is this divinely-appointed role to be revived? In recent years Jewish insularity has been challenged by a new Christian theological development. In the late 1960s a new theological initiative was launched in Latin America. In 1968 a Latin American Bishops' Conference (CELAM) was held at Medellin, Colombia; this gathering was followed by a second conference in 1971 in Santiago, Chile, and a third at Publea, Mexico in 1979. At these meetings Christian participants focused on the injustice done to the poor in their own countries. Confronting modern forms of oppression and exploitation, they looked to the Scriptural sources for a discernment of God's saving action in the world. In particular they attempted to show that the God of the Hebrew Bible is He who is on the side of the enslaved in all societies. In this return to biblical sources, Christian liberationists have redefined for modern society the message of the Exodus as well as the prophetic tradition.

According to these liberationists, the biblical account portrays the Israelites as an oppressed people. Suffering torment, their complaints led to new burdens rather than relief. But the Israelites were not alone: God heard the groaning of the people and remembered the covenant. Moreover, God declared that the people would be liberated from their bondage. Moses was delegated to lead the people out of Egypt, and after many trials this was accomplished. For these Christians this story of hope is of great solace. It is reassuring to read that God does not remain aloof from situations of human history, that He acted against Pharoah, and that Israel's liberation was not simply from individual sin and guilt. Rather, freedom implies liberation from oppressive political and economic structures. It is clear then that God has a real concern with life on earth, in times past and now.

This biblical narrative therefore shows that God is loving and takes sides with the down-trodden. This means that He is against the Pharoahs of today's world, the modern

3

exploiters. In this context liberation theologians emphasize the scriptural message that God demands justice. This theme is a constant feature of prophetic Judaism. The prophet Jeremiah, for example, declared:

> Woe to him who builds his house by unrighteousness,
> and its upper rooms by injustice.
> Who makes his neighbour serve him for nothing,
> and does not give him his wages;
> who says, 'I will build myself a great house
> with spacious upper rooms,'
> And cuts out windows for it,
> paneling it with cedar, and painting it with vermilion (Jer. 22: 13–15)

Referring to the practice of justice and right, and the defence of the poor, Jeremiah posed the question: 'Is not this to know me? says the Lord' (Jer. 22:16). In this rhetorical question Jeremiah explained that knowing God entails acts of righteousness. To know God is not to engage in ritual acts nor to subscribe to correct religious beliefs. To know God is to do justice. This conviction adds depth to a later passage in Jeremiah in which God's new covenant is described. In this covenant 'no longer shall each man teach his neighbour and each his brother, saying, "know the Lord" for they shall all know me' (Jer. 31:34). Here an explicit equation is made between knowing God and doing justice, which transforms the nature of the new covenant.

No only, according to liberation theologians, is the knowledge of God predicated on doing justice, but the worship of God also entails acts of righteousness. Here the words of Amos express the Hebrew conviction that without justice there can be no authentic worship:

> I hate, I despise your feasts,
> and I take no delight in your solemn assemblies . . .
> Take away from me the noise of your songs;
> to the melody of your harps I will not listen.
> But let justice roll down like waters,
> and righteousness like an ever flowing stream (Amos 5:21, 23–24)

In formulating a Christian theology of liberation, and in exploring the role of the Church in contemporary society, South American liberationists have therefore relied heavily on the central biblical ideas of freedom derived from the book of Exodus and the prophetic writings – in this way they have revitalized and readapted the teachings of the Hebrew Scriptures. This Christian initiative is of profound importance for Jewish-Christian dialogue: in contemporary society Christian liberation theology can act as a clarion call, drawing the Jewish nation back to its biblical heritage. God's deliverance of His chosen people from bondage in Egypt and His moral commandments as recorded in Scripture thus set the agenda for Jewish-Christian encounter in a post-Holocaust world.

This study begins, in Chapter 1, with an exposition of the central themes found in my book, *On Earth as it is in Heaven: Jews, Christians and Liberation Theology*. That work, published in 1987, was the first extended examination of the challenge of Christian liberation theology for Jewish thought. In it I examined the ways in which Christian liberation theologians have focused on the themes of the Exodus, the prophetic cry for justice and the understanding of Jesus as a liberator in presenting their view of Christian action and commitment in contemporary society. Breaking with previous Christian conceptions of Jesus' spiritual role in bringing about God's Kingdom, they have stressed instead the realization of a more humane society. For Jews, I argue, this emphasis on the concrete dimension of faith is also vital. As with Christian liberation theology, the traditional Jewish hope is for God's rule on earth. Christian liberation theology, I maintain, can thus serve to reawaken the Jewish community to its divinely-appointed universalistic task.

In Chapter 2 we shall examine the second Jewish response to liberation theology by the American Jewish theologian Marc H. Ellis. In his book *Toward a Jewish Liberation Theology*, Ellis maintains that Jews must transcend their current ethnocentric concerns and reach out to all those who are enslaved. In today's society, he argues, it is imperative that the Jewish community champion the cause of those who, like the Jews of previous centuries, are undergoing hardship and deprivation. In particular, he is concerned with the plight of the Palestinians who are anxious to establish a homeland. It is vital, he emphasizes, that Jews who were once victims do not become victimisers. Paralleling my presentation in *On Earth as it is in Heaven*, his book looks to Christian liberation theology as a framework for revitalizing Jewish faith in the modern world.

In our two books, Marc Ellis and I advocated the formulation of a contemporary Jewish liberation theology. In Chapter 3 I discuss a number of responses by both Jewish and Christian theologians to this initiative. Some writers such as Judd Kruger Levingston, Norman Solomon, and Richard L. Rubenstein have offered a number of criticisms of such a development. Other writers, however, including Leonardo Boff, Michael Lerner, Rosemary Radford Ruether, Pablo Richard, Julio de Santa Ana, and Dorothee Sölle have been much more sympathetic. In their view a Jewish theology of liberation could fruitfully confront such issues as the state of Israel, the Palestinian question, and the problem of Jewish empowerment.

In the light of such encouragement, the concluding chapter outlines a number of central elements of the Jewish faith which could serve as building blocks for constructing a Jewish theology of liberation. Of paramount importance is the motif of the Exodus as well as its embodiment in the Passover celebration. A further resource is the prophetic tradition, redolent with the themes of justice and freedom. So too the motifs of God's Kingdom on earth, Judaism's focus on moral principles, and the stress on ethical behaviour constitute essential elements. As Jews stand on the threshold of the twenty-first century the task of formulating such a theology, which could deal with the problems of the modern world, has never been more urgent.

1 Christian Liberation Theology and Jewish Thought

By the early 1980s liberation theology had made a major impact on theological circles in both the Third and the First World. Yet in the Jewish community no attention was being paid to this vitally important new movement. Instead Jewish scholars and theologians were preoccupied with traditional concerns and modes of scholarship. Given such ignorance, Phillip Scharper, the head of Orbis Books in Maryknoll, New York (the primary publishing house for liberation theology in English) asked me to write a book about the common ground between liberation theology and Jewish thought. In 1987 *On Earth as it is in Heaven: Jews, Christians and Liberation Theology* appeared. In that volume I attempted to illustrate the common connections between Jewish thought and Christian liberationism. This study served as the starting point for the debate that has continued for several years. Essentially my book maps out a number of crucial theological issues and areas of overlap.

A New Christology

In *On Earth as it is in Heaven* I stressed that, through the centuries, Jesus has been understood as the risen Christ who sits at the right hand of the Father. The doctrines of the Incarnation and the Trinity have been central tenets of the Christian faith, and this perhaps more than anything else has made fruitful Jewish-Christian dialogue difficult, if not impossible. Yet today there is a possibility for Jews and Christians to find a meeting point, since liberation theologians repeatedly emphasize that their concern is not to theorize abstractly about Christological doctrines. Such

7

traditional reflection, they believe, has been misguided since it has tended to obscure the figure of Christ. Christ has frequently been reduced to sublime abstraction: this has led to a spiritual conception of the Son of God divorced from Jesus' concrete historicity.

Such a theoretically abstract presentation of Christ has given rise to the view that Jesus was a pacifist who loved all human beings and died on behalf of all people to free them from sin. According to liberation theologians, such an emphasis distorts the real nature of Jesus in that it exempts him from history and uses Christianity as a support for ideologies espousing peace and order (Jon Sobrino, 1978, xvi). Liberation theologians further point out that if Christ is seen as the absolute in abstract terms, earthly matters tend to be neglected; in particular, the emphasis on the absoluteness of Christ can bring about an unquestioning acceptance of the social and political status quo (Sobrino, 1978, xvii).

In the light of these objections to traditional Christian speculation, liberation theologians insist that the historical Jesus should be the starting point for Christological reflection. Gustavo Gutiérrez, for example, urges that Jesus be viewed historically:

> To approach the man Jesus of Nazareth, in whom God was made flesh, to penetrate not only in his teaching, but also in his life, what it is that gives his word an immediate, concrete context, is a task which more and more needs to be undertaken (Gutiérrez, 1973, 226).

Following this impetus, liberation theology stresses the Jesus of history over the Jesus of faith. In particular liberationists see a structural similarity between the situation of Jesus' time and that of the modern world. Oppression and persecution in contemporary society, as in first-century Palestine, they believe, are contrary to the divine plan for humankind. In the gospels Jesus initiated a programme of liberation: his struggle against the Jewish authorities illustrates the conflict that any project of liberation will provoke. The historical Jesus thus clarifies the chief elements of Christological faith. By following his life and cause in one's own life, the truth of Jesus emerges. Leonardo Boff explains: 'Jesus does not present himself as the explanation of reality; he presents himself as an urgent demand for the transformation of that reality (Boff, 1978, 279). By offering a critique of humanity and society, Jesus points the way to the fulfilment of the kingdom of God (Boff, 1978, 280).

For Jews, liberation theology thus offers a new orientation to Jesus. For 20 centuries Jews and Christians have been unable to find common theological ground. Instead of attempting to build a bridge with Christianity, Jews have repudiated Christian claims about Jesus' divinity and Christians have denounced Jews for their unwillingness to accept Christ as their Saviour. The doctrines of the Trinity and the Incarnation and the understanding of Jesus as the Messiah have separated the two traditions and have served as stumbling blocks to fruitful interfaith encounter.

Today, however, liberation theology offers a profoundly different direction to Christian thought. Unlike theologians of the past, liberation theologians are not concerned to analyse Jesus' dual nature as God and man; abstract speculation about the central issues of traditional Christology have been set aside. Instead, liberation theology focuses on the historical Jesus as the starting point for Christian reflection. Jon Sobrino writes:

> Our Christology will . . . avoid abstractionism and the attendant danger of manipulating the Christ event. The history of the Church shows, from its very beginning . . . that any focusing on the Christ of faith will jeopardize the very essence of the Christian faith if it neglects the historical Jesus (Sobrino, 1978, 9).

What is of crucial significance for Jewish-Christian dialogue is the primary emphasis on understanding Jesus as a first-century Palestinian Jew. It is the flesh-and-blood Jesus of history who is of fundamental importance for liberation theologians; the concrete preaching and acting of Jesus provide the basis for the formulation of Christian theology.

The historical context of the gospels is in this way reclaimed for Christians, and Jesus' teaching in the New Testament is related directly to God's design as recorded in the Hebrew Scriptures. In particular, Jesus is viewed as following in the footsteps of the great prophets of ancient Israel. Ignacio Ellacuría insists that prophecy in the Hebrew Scriptures and Jesus' mission in the New Testament must be related:

> The prophecy of the Old Testament takes on its full ascendant import only in terms of what Jesus himself represents. By the same token the meaning of Jesus himself would escape us if we disregarded the history of prophecy (Ellacuría, 1976, 23).

From a historical standpoint, then, the picture of Jesus that emerges from the gospel narratives is inextricably connected to his Jewish background. The consequence of this for Jews is profound, for it opens the way to a fresh vision of Jesus' mission. His criticism of the religious establishment, like that of the pre-exilic prophets, should not be understood as a rejection of Judaism but as a call to the nation to return to the God of their ancestors. Seen in this manner, Jesus' teaching stands in the tradition of the ethical prophets of ancient Israel. We must turn to the prophetic books of the Bible to find the crucial links that relate Jesus to his Jewish past. In this context Jews can recognize Jesus as following the prophetic tradition even though they cannot say with the Christian liberation theologian that Jesus is 'God of God, light of light, very God of very God, begotten not made, being of one substance with the Father.'

Jesus as Prophet

Continuing my presentation of the interconnections between Christian liberation theology and Jewish thought, I noted in *On Earth as it is in Heaven* that, for liberation theologians, Jesus belongs to the line of prophecy in ancient Israel which began with the eighth-century prophets and continued through the post-exilic period. Such a view of Jesus is grounded in the New Testament. In the gospels Jesus transcended prophecy, but remained within the prophetic tradition. According to Ellacuría, the important thing to note here is that the people who lived with Jesus situated him in the prophetic line (Ellacuría, 1976). While their theological purposes may have differed greatly, the texts of Matthew 16:14 and Mark 8:27–33 clearly show that the people around Jesus placed him in the line of Elijah, Jeremiah, and John the Baptist. In short, they saw him as one of the nation's great prophets. It is in and through the prophetic dimension that the people and Jesus' disciples moved towards an understanding of who and what Jesus was in his ultimate reality. Hence, one cannot grasp the ultimate reality of Jesus' life apart from his life as a prophet.

By placing himself in the line of the prophetic tradition, Jesus showed how anxious he was to call the people back to the true worship of God, and his words and actions testify to his dedication to compassion and loving-kindness. In Scripture Jesus healed the sick on the Sabbath in violation of Pharisaic law; in addition he conspicuously turned his attention to the lowly, to sinners, to children and to foreigners.

> All these people suffer from a lack of something: health, life-prospects, prestige in the eyes of the 'just', abilities, acceptance among Jews. They are all marginalized. And if they have any value, they cannot express it: the poor because nobody assists them or does them justice: the others because 'religious society' punctiliously excluded the outcast: Jesus addresses himself to all the marginalized people, doubly oppressed by human egotism in general and by the 'religious' structure in particular. He begins his liberation by giving value to their persons. They too are *human* beings, but oppressed (Sobrino, 1978, 50–1).

In the case of those who were most sorely in need, Jesus was able to illustrate the love and concern that we are all required to exhibit to our neighbours.

Jesus established fellowship with all those who were at the margin of society; he continually took the side of the

weak who were ostracized and condemned by the general
public. His approach was to accept all these people. For
Jesus they stood within the pale of salvation; he conversed
with prostitutes and welcomed outcasts; he ate with the
dishonest tax-collector Zacceus; it is almost certain that he
numbered freedom fighters among his disciples and women
were among his closest associates. For befriending such
individuals, Jesus was characterized as a 'glutton and
drunkard, a friend of tax collectors and sinners' (Matt.
11:19). Nevertheless, Jesus asserted God's love for all
humankind, even the wicked and ungrateful. It was these,
he declared, who were sick and in need of a doctor: 'Those
who are well,' he stated, 'have no need of a physician, but
those who are sick; I came not to call the righteous, but
sinners' (Mark 2:17). As Luke recorded, Jesus came 'to
seek and save the lost' (Luke 19:10).

The response to this solidarity with outsiders was
hostile: Jesus was insulted and defamed. He was called the
companion of wicked people. He was accused of being a
heretic, a madman, and a tool of the devil. Gibellini
explains:

> It is through this sort of love and these mediating conditions
> that he senses the meaning of God's kingdom and liberation
> from the oppressive frameworks that create discrimination
> between human beings. One's neighbours are not just those
> who hold the same faith or belong to the same family or race,
> one's neighbours are all human beings (Gibellini, 1980, 111).

The figure of Jesus that emerges from these encounters is
that of a man who gave himself to others, especially to
those who suffered. His was a love that united all peoples:
'Whatever you wish that men would do to you,' he
declared, 'do so to them; for this is the law and the prophets' (Matt. 7:12). In the Sermon on the Mount Jesus
emphasized in prophetic fashion that loving-kindness is
the cardinal principle of human action, a total giving that
demands exertion, generosity and responsibility. Such
love, he contended, must extend even to one's enemies:

> You have heard that it was said, 'An eye for an eye and a
> tooth for a tooth.'
> But I say to you. Do not resist one who is evil.
> But if any one strikes you on the right cheek, turn to him the
> other also;
> And if any one would sue you and take your coat, let him
> have your cloak as well;
> And if any one forces you to go one mile, go with him two
> miles (Matt. 5:38–41).

For Jesus, devotion to God necessarily entails a selfless
love for others. Thus when one of the scribes asked him
which commandment is the most important, Jesus replied:

> The first is 'Hear, O Israel: The Lord our God, the Lord is
> one; and you shall love the Lord your God with all your heart,
> and with all your soul, and with all your mind, and with all
> your strength.' The second is this, 'You shall love your neigh-
> bour as yourself' (Mark 12:29–31).

Salvation, Jesus contended, was decided on the basis of
love for one's neighbour: When he was asked what must
be done to attain eternal life, Jesus answered first by quoting the moral commandments (Mark 10:17–22). Such an
orientation echoed the prophetic insistence on righteousness. By removing the emphasis on the legalistic and ritual-
istic dimensions of the Jewish tradition, Jesus illustrated
that the love of God must necessarily keep one pointed in
the direction of love for other human beings.

Jesus thus condemned all malevolent thoughts and
actions. In the Sermon on the Mount, he decried hatred
and anger:

> You have heard that it was said to the men of old, 'You shall
> not kill, and whoever kills shall be liable to judgment.'
> But I say to you that everyone who is angry with his brother
> shall be liable to judgment (Matt 5:21–22).

Jesus' words hence recalled the great prophets of ancient
Israel, and like them he used graphic images to emphasize
the importance of love. In his parable about the Good
Samaritan, he pointed out that love for one's neighbour

must include all people; neighbourliness knows no boundaries of race or class (Luke 10:29–37).

In the life and ministry of Jesus as recorded in the gospels, we can see the bonds that link him to his Jewish past. Like Amos, Isaiah, and Jeremiah, as well as the post-exilic prophets who followed them, Jesus rebuked the people for turning away from God. The Hebrew prophets' experience was of a God so concerned with human social justice that he was compelled to pour out his wrath on Israel for her infidelity to the Torah. The prophets attacked the exploitation of the poor by the rich because God demands not sacrifice but human justice; they condemned the people for turning the worship of God into a mechanical process divorced from the offering of a heart committed to acts of loving-kindness. So too, Jesus condemned the leaders of the people for their hardheartedness, hypocrisy, and injustice. Love of God, Jesus insisted, must involve love for all peoples.

This vision of Jesus as a prophet of Israel, calling the people back to the true worship of God, is at the heart of Christian liberation theology. This prophetic understanding of Jesus should make it possible for the Jew to gain a sympathetic insight into Jesus' ministry. His attack on the scribes and Pharisees can be seen, not as a rejection of the Torah, but as a prophetic denunciation of a corrupt religious establishment. Such a concept of Jesus should enable both Jews and Christians to set aside previous Christological barriers to interfaith dialogue and concentrate on a shared prophetic vision. Instead of rejecting Jesus as a blasphemous heretic, the emphasis of liberation theology can enable the Jew to see in Jesus' life a reflection of the prophetic ideals of Israel.

Christianity and God's Kingdom

'My kingdom is not of this world' (John 18:36). In my earlier book I argued that on the basis of this claim, traditional Christianity redefined the concept of the Kingdom of God: the fervent Jewish expectation of a total transformation of the world was replaced by a spiritualized and individualized hope for immortal, celestial life. The reign of God was no longer understood as a Jewish hope for the reordering of earthly life; rather it appeared as a heavenly promise that offered salvation for the individual. Within this framework, the temporal world was understood as having only preparatory value. The eternal realm by contrast was seen as the dimension of life in which the Christian could reach ultimate fulfilment and happiness. Given such an otherworldly outlook, Christian existence was significant only in that it could help the individual to achieve and express the religious and moral virtues that belong to the Christian life.

In the history of the Christian transformation of the Jewish doctrine of the Kingdom of God, Paul was the principle witness. For the Palestinians of the Jesus-movement, the crucifixion of their Messiah presented a deeply perplexing problem. But for Paul this event posed no difficulty; instead Jesus' death on the cross revealed the divine plan. 'I have been crucified with Christ,' he declared, 'it is no longer I who live, but Christ who lives in me; and the life I now live in the flesh I live by faith in the Son of God, who loved me and gave himself for me' (Gal. 2:20).

Paul's message was that God himself had entered through Christ into human sufferings. According to Paul, from the time of Adam sin had ruled over humankind: 'Therefore as sin came into the world through one man and death through sin, so death spread to all men because all men sinned' (Rom. 5:12). To save humanity from the bonds of sin God sent Christ to die in expiation.

It was to the sinner, then, that Paul addressed his message. All have sinned and all are thereby liable to punishment. For this reason Jesus died to free humankind:

> While we were still weak, at the right time Christ died for the ungodly. Why, one will hardly die for the righteous man – though perhaps for a good man one will dare even to die. But God shows his love for us in that while we were yet sinners Christ died for us (Rom. 5:6–8).

Under the influence of Pauline thought, the Christian faith was able to break with its Jewish origins and appeal to the masses as a spiritual religion unencumbered by feelings of national loyalty.

This concept of an internalized and spiritualized Kingdom of God has worked throughout history as a deterrent for Christian action. Today, however, liberation theologians reject such an interpretation of the role of the Church. Christianity, they maintain, embodies an ethic to transform the world; the gospel must galvanize the believer into action. José Míguez Bonino writes:

> God builds his Kingdom from and within human history in its entirety; his action is a constant call and challenge to man. Man's response is realized in the concrete arena of history with its economic, political, ideological options. Faith is not a different history but a dynamic, a motivation, and in its eschatological horizon, a transforming invitation (Míguez Bonino, 1975, 138).

For liberation theologians, historical events – economic, political and social – are intimately connected with the Kingdom of God. 'The elimination of misery and exploitation,' writes Gutiérrez, 'is a sign of the coming of the Kingdom' (Gutiérrez, 1973, 167). Concern for the Kingdom therefore involves a commitment to the future of humanity on earth. To seek the reign of God is to accept the duty of being involved in human history. Such a commitment 'allows no basis for a spirituality of evasion which is uninterested in the problems of those among whom we live' (Davies, 1976, 21).

God's Kingdom is hence understood as intimately connected with the establishment of justice on earth. Liberation theologians emphasize that this worldly concept of the Kingdom is deeply rooted in the Hebrew Scriptures. Within this biblical context liberation theologians explicate the meaning of the Kingdom of God in the life and teaching of Jesus. From the beginning of his ministry, Jesus preached that the Kingdom of God had come. For Jesus the coming of the Kingdom was a process that would culminate in a final eschatological climax at the end of time. The end of the world began with Jesus' ministry; he ushered in the Kingdom that is to be consummated in the parousia. The breakthrough of the Kingdom entailed a complete restructuring of the old order. This was the task that Jesus began. The announcement of the Kingdom was therefore a call by Jesus to embark on the project of liberation. Thus Gutiérrez writes:

> Jesus was only turning to the great prophetic line which required 'mercy and not sacrifice', 'contrite hearts and not holocausts' . . . For the prophets this demand was inseparable from the dununciation of social injustice and from the vigorous assertion that God is known only by doing justice (Gutiérrez, 1973, 230).

The growth and ultimate fulfilment of the Kingdom rests on a struggle against exploitation, alienation, oppression, and persecution. It embraces all: the world, society, and the individual. This totality is to be transformed through the activity that God has initiated through Christ but not yet completed.

Within this unfolding of God's eschatological scheme, liberation theologians maintain that Christians have a vital role. It is the responsibility of each person to engage in the quest for the liberation of the oppressed. All Christians are obliged to offer assistance to this task not only in the religious and spiritual domain, but also in the spheres of politics, economics, and culture. 'It is not enough to say that doing so is a condition for salvation; it is the very coming of the Kingdom in its temporal form' (Bigo, 1977, 131). The way of the Kingdom implies the building of a just society. Gutiérrez notes that a situation of injustice is incompatible with the Kingdom:

> The building of a just society has worth in terms of the Kingdom, or in more current phraseology, to participate in the process of liberation is already in a certain sense, a salvific work (Gutiérrez, 1973, 72).

Entrance into the Kingdom is open only to those who

practise justice and distribute to the poor whatever they have over and above their own needs.

The heart of the gospel message is subversive; it embodies the Israelite hope in the end of the domination of some human beings over others. The struggle for the establishment of God's Kingdom involves the overthrow of established powers: political involvement is imperative. To know God is to be concerned for the creation of a new order regulated by the principle of love.

> Our hope may refer to the Kingdom, to the second coming of Christ, but it begins here and now, in this society in which I happen to live and for those whose transformation – humanization – I am inescapably responsible . . . loving one's neighbour, which is the first commandment by definition, today means working to change the structures that can destroy my neighbour, the people, the poor (Echegoyen, 1971, 464ff.).

For liberation theologians such change involves the eradication of poverty, which is incompatible with a Kingdom of love and justice. Some theologians even go as far as to advocate the necessity of violent revolution as a means of altering the economic structures of society.

The writings of these theologians express a common conviction that the rights of the poor must be upheld in a quest for the liberation of the oppressed. Peace, justice, love and freedom are dominating motifs in their understanding of the coming of God's Kingdom. Breaking with traditional Christian theology, liberation theologians emphasize that these are not internal attitudes; they are social realities, which need to be implemented in human history. Gutiérrez eloquently formulates this shift away from the values of the past:

> A poorly understood spiritualization has often made us forget the human consequences of the eschatological promises and the power to transform unjust social structures which they imply. The elimination of misery and exploitation is a sign of the coming of the Kingdom (Gutiérrez, 1973, 167).

Thus the Kingdom of God, contrary to what many Christians believe, does not signify something that is outside this world. Each individual must make an effort to bring about a new order, a mission based on Jesus' actions and teachings as recorded in the gospels.

Jewish Theology and the Kingdom

In *On Earth as it is in Heaven* I stressed that what is of central importance for Christian-Jewish encounter is the liberationist's insistence that the coming of the Kingdom involves individual participation in the creation of a new world. Though Judaism rejects the Christian claim that Jesus ushered in the period of messianic redemption, Jews have steadfastly adhered to the belief that God is a supreme ruler who calls all people to join in bringing about the Kingdom of God on earth. This understanding was a central theological motif of the Hebrew Scriptures; in later rabbinic literature, this vision of the human role in bringing about God's Kingdom was further elaborated. According to the rabbis, the Kingdom of God would take place in this world: it will be established by human obedience to the divine will. The Kingdom of God consists in a complete moral order on earth – the reign of trust, righteousness, and holiness among all nations. The fulfilment of this concept would ultimately rest with the coming of the Messiah. Nevertheless, it is the duty of humanity to participate in the creation of a better world in anticipation of the messianic redemption. In the words of the rabbis, 'Man is a co-worker with God in the work of creation' (Shab. 119b).

According to rabbinic theology, humanity is the centre of creation, for it is only human beings among all created beings who can through righteousness make the Kingdom glorious (Agadoth Shir Hashirim, 18, 61). In rabbinic midrash the view is expressed that God's kingship did not come into operation until human beings were created:

> When the Holy One, blessed be he, consulted the Torah as to the creation of the world, he answered, 'Master of the world, if there be no host, over whom will the King reign, and if there be no peoples praising him, where is the glory of the King?' (Pirke de Rabbi Eliezer, Ch. 3).

Only human beings, then, can make the Kingdom glorious; God wanted to reign over free agents, who could act as God's partners in perfecting the world. But God requires obedience to the ways of righteousness and justice:

> You are my lovers and friends. 'You walk in my ways,' God declared to Israel. 'As the Omnipotent is merciful and gracious, long-suffering and abundant in goodness so be ye . . . feeding the hungry, giving drink to the thirsty, clothing the naked, ransoming the captives, and marrying the orphans.' (Agadoth Shir Hashirim, 18, 61).

The idea of the Kingdom was conceived by the rabbis as ethical in character.

> If, then, the Kingdom of God was thus originally intended to be in the midst of men and for men at large (as represented by Adam), if its first preachers were, like Abraham, ex-heathens, who addressed themselves to heathens, if, again, the essence of their preaching was righteousness and justice, and if lastly, the Kingdom does not mean a hierarchy, but any form of government conducted on the principles of righteousness, holiness, justice, and charitableness, then we may safely maintain that the Kingdom of God, as taught by Judaism in one of its aspects, is universal in its aims (Schechter, 1961, 93).

According to the Hebrew Scriptures, God's identification with morality is absolute. In the prophetic writings the primacy of ethical behaviour is asserted, and this emphasis continued throughout rabbinic literature. Believing themselves to possess an authentic oral tradition as to the meaning of Scripture, the rabbis expounded and amplified the ethical injunctions of the Bible. Thus throughout rabbinic sources, the rabbis sought to ensure that God's moral precepts are upheld. In this light the Jewish people are acceptable to God only when they fulfil the commandments of the Torah. Hence we read in the midrash:

> It is like a king who said to his wife, 'Deck yourself with all your ornaments that you may be acceptable to me.' So God says to Israel, 'Be distinguished by the commandments that you may be acceptable to me.' As it says, 'Fair art thou,

my beloved, when thou are acceptable to me.' (Sifre Deut., Wa'ethanan, S 36 fin., f 75b).

For the rabbis, morality and religion form a single, inseparable whole. Faith in God entails the obligation to be good, for God has commanded that the people follow the divine moral dictates. This view was eloquently illustrated in rabbinic lore:

> It happened once that R. Reuben was in Tiberius on the Sabbath, and a philosopher asked him: 'Who is the most hateful man in the world?' He replied, 'The man who denies his Creator.' 'How so?' said the philosopher. R. Reuben answered, 'Honour thy father and thy mother, thou shalt do no murder, thou shalt not commit adultery, thou shalt not steal, thou shalt not bear false witness against thy neighbour, thou shalt not covet.' No man denies the derivative (i.e. the separate commandments) until he has previously denied the Root (i.e. God), and no man sins unless he has denied Him who commanded him not to commit that sin (T. Shebu'ot III, 6).

Moral precepts are grounded in the will of God; in this light the Torah serves as the blueprint for moral action, and it is through the admonitions of the rabbis in midrashic and talmudic sources that the Jewish people are encouraged to put the teachings of the Law into effect in their everyday life. According to the rabbis the Kingdom of God is inconsistent with injustice and social misery; the effort to bring about the perfection of the world so that God will reign in majesty is a human responsibility. Jewish ethics as enshrined in the Bible and in rabbinic literature were thus inextricably related to the coming of God's Kingdom. Throughout biblical and rabbinic literature, Jews were encouraged to strive for the highest concept of life, in which the rule of truth, righteousness, and holiness would be established among humankind. Such a desire is the eternal hope of God's people – a longing for His Kingdom as expressed in the daily liturgy of the synagogue.

Here we can see the point of intersection between the Jewish faith and Christian liberation theology. For both

Jews and liberation theologians the coming of the Kingdom
in which God's heavenly rule will be made manifest is a
process in which all human beings have a role. The coming
of the Kingdom requires a struggle for the reign of justice
and righteousness on earth. The Kingdom is not – as it is
in traditional Christianity – an internalized, spiritualized,
otherworldly concept. Rather it involves human activity in
a historical context. Drawing on the Old and New Testaments, liberation theologians have attempted to demon-
strate the tasks Christians must undertake in the building
of the Kingdom. Similarly, the rabbis elaborated the teaching of the Torah about human partnership with God in
bringing about God's rule. For both faiths, the moral life
is at the centre of the unfolding of God's plan for humanity.
Such a shared vision should serve to unite Jews and Christians in the joint undertaking of transforming our imperfect
world in anticipation of the divine promise of the eschatological fulfilment at the end of time.

The Exodus and Christian Liberation

In my book I pointed out that for liberation theologians
Jesus is the liberator who paves the way for the realization
of the Kingdom of God on earth. In presenting this message of hope liberation theologians repeatedly emphasize
the centrality of the Exodus from Egypt.

> The Exodus experience is paradigmatic. It remains vital and
> contemporary due to similar historical experiences which the
> People of God undergo . . . It structures our faith in the gift
> of the Father's love. In Christ and through the Spirit, men
> are becoming one in the very heart of history (Gutiérrez,
> 1973, 159).

Thus these Christian theologians look to the history of
the Jewish people for inspiration in their struggle against
exploitation and oppression in contemporary society, and
this divine act of redemption of the Israelite nation provides a basis for a critique of traditional Christian thought
and modern society.

In Egypt the ancient Israelites were exploited and oppressed. Elsa Tamez notes that this experience of oppression involved a degradation so severe that it caused the people to turn to God for deliverance (Tamez, 1982). The Egyptians overwhelmed the Hebrew slaves with work; they 'made their lives bitter with hard service, in mortar and brick, and in all kinds of work in the field; in all their work they made them serve with rigour' (Exod. 1: 14). Such affliction causes the people to cry out to God for liberation. In response God decreed:

> I have seen the affliction of my people who are in Egypt, and have heard their cry because of their taskmasters; I know their sufferings, and I have come down to deliver them out of the hand of the Egyptians (Exod. 3:7–8).

From this act of deliverance liberation theologians derive a message of hope: if God was on the side of the poor in ancient Israel, surely He still takes side with the downtrodden. Thus if God has a bias today it is with the poor and oppressed. This means that God is against the Pharaohs of the modern world. Who are these Pharaohs? They are:

> the tiny minority at home who are in collusion against the great majority; they are the churches and churchpersons who give support to such oligarchies; and they are the rich and powerful from other nations who keep national oligarchies in power, thereby becoming complicit in the ongoing exploitation of the poor (Brown, 1978, 89–90).

In the view of liberation theologians God works to liberate those who are oppressed by socio-economic structures that are evil, exploitative, and unjust; those who seek to be co-workers with God in creating a just society must side with whatever forces are working for the liberation of humankind. According to these writers, the Exodus was not simply an event in the history of the Jewish people; instead it evokes a deep response on the part of the descendants of those who were liberated.

The word [Exodus] was 'recharged' with fresh meanings by

successive hermeneutical re-readings up to the time that it was fixed permanently as expressing a whole world-view in the Exodus account in its present form (Croatto, 1981, 14).

The profundity of the Exodus therefore consists in its significance for later generations; the past holds a promise for those who understand its relevance. The Exodus is fraught with meaning. For liberation theologians it is an account of the liberation of oppressed peoples. They believe it is possible to understand the plight of those who are presently afflicted from the perspective of the biblical Exodus – the situation of peoples in economic, political, social, or cultural 'bondage' (Croatto, 1981, 15).

In this context liberation theologians stress Moses' crucial role in the process of liberation. Enrique Dussel, for example, begins his study of the history and theology of liberation by focusing on Moses' call to lead his people out of captivity (Dussel, 1976). Moses fled to the desert because he killed an Egyptian. He lived comfortably as a herdsman with his wife, his father-in-law, and his flocks. But one day he heard God speak to him out of a bush. 'Moses, Moses,' God cried:

> I have seen the affliction of my people who are in Egypt, and have heard their cry because of their taskmasters; I know their sufferings, and I have come down to deliver them out of the hand of the Egyptians . . . Come, I will send you to Pharaoh that you may bring forth my people, the sons of Israel, out of Egypt (Exod. 3:7–10).

Liberation theologians also utilize the Exodus narrative to explain that God guides the destiny of the persecuted. In the flight from Egypt the Bible stresses that it was God who led the people. God did not take them out by the way of the land of the Philistines although that was near, for God said, 'lest the people repent when they see war, and return to Egypt. But God led the people round by the way of the wilderness towards the Red Sea' (Exod. 13:17–18). When the Egyptian army attempted to capture the Israelites, God intervened and they were saved (Exod. 14:24–28).

Once Israel had crossed the Red Sea, God sustained them in their wanderings: God gave them sweet water at Marah (Exod. 15:22, 25), sent them manna and quail in the desert (Exod. 16:4–36), gave them safe passage through the Transjordan (Num. 21:21–24; Deut. 2:26–37), and delivered the Amorite kings into the hands of the Israelites (Deut. 3:12–17). Not only did God deliver and protect the people, He also led them to their own land where they were no longer oppressed. Before Moses' death, God proclaimed to Joshua: 'I myself will be with you' (Deut. 31:23). God promised to be with Joshua as God was with Moses (Josh. 1:5).

The conquest was thus the second stage of God's deliverance, and even the prostitute of Jericho knew that God would take the side of the people as had happened in the past: 'I know that the Lord has given you the land . . . We have heard how the Lord dried up the water of the Red Sea before you when you came out of Egypt' (Josh. 2:9–10).

According to some liberation theologians, a central element of the process of liberation is the use of violence. Paradoxically love and violence are interconnected:

> Love can be violent when the loved object cannot be retained or recovered except by force . . . The history of the Exodus is eminently instructive in this respect. God acts with vigour . . . 'I will bring you out from under the burdens of the Egyptians' (Exod. 6:6); 'I know that the king of Egypt will not let you go unless compelled by a mighty hand' (Exod. 3:10) (Croatto, 1981, 29).

The Exodus is thus a pivotal event for liberation theology; it is regarded as the salvation experience *par excellence*. To the Hebrew mind, salvation involves a historical experience on the political and social planes; God is viewed as Saviour because He acts in human history. In the unfolding of the divine plan of deliverance, God was revealed through Moses, and, as J. Severino Croatto notes, 'Moses had to assume that historical and personal vocation to freedom' (Croatto, 1981, 28).

Similarly, Jesus is viewed by liberation theologians as an

emissary of God; he is the typological correlate of Moses. The Exodus is a central event in the life of the Jewish nation, and it serves as a fundamental model of divine activity in liberation theology. The departure from Egypt:

> is much more than a mere image designed to enrich theological representations; it becomes the primeval and fundamental happening of the history of divine revelation itself. The Exodus comes to constitute the prototype of divine revelation, the privileged moment in which God once manifested himself and now continues to do the same (Fierro, 1977, 141).

The Jewish Passover

As we have seen, the experience of the Exodus is typologically significant for liberation theologians; it is a paradigm of divine liberation of the oppressed and persecuted. In my book I pointed out that just as the Exodus is a key element in liberation theology so it has been central to the self-understanding of the Jewish people throughout the centuries. In the biblical period, details of the Exodus are recorded in cultic sayings in the Psalms, in wisdom literature, and by the prophets. After the exile the Exodus continued to play a dominant role in the Jewish faith. In particular, the festival of Passover was regarded as crucially important in the religious life of the people.

The Passover *seder* envisages the Exodus experience as a symbol of freedom from oppression, and the whole of the *Haggadah* is pervaded by the image of God as the Saviour of humankind. For this reason the Passover service beings with an ancient formulaic invitation to those who hunger or are in need to participate in the festival:

> This is the bread of affliction that our fathers ate in the land of Egypt. All who hunger, let them come and eat: all who are in need, let them come and celebrate the Passover. Now we are here – next year we shall be free men.

Any Jew who sits down to the Passover meal and is oblivious to the call of those who are in want has missed the meaning of the celebration.

During the service the leader displays the unleavened bread to stimulate the curiosity of the youngsters at the meal. It is then the turn of the youngest child to ask about the nature of the Passover festivities. The entire ritual of the *seder* hinges on these inquiries. In reply the leader recites the narrative of the Exodus stressing the themes of liberation and freedom from oppression.

> We were Pharaoh's servants in Egypt; and the Lord our God brought us out thereof with a mighty hand and an outstretched arm. Now, had not the Holy One brought out our fathers from Egypt, then we and our children and our children's children would be enslaved to Pharaoh in Egypt. Wherefore, even were we all wise men, all men of understanding, all advanced in years, all men with knowledge of the Torah, it would yet be our duty to recount the story of the coming forth from Egypt; and all who recount at length the story of the coming forth from Egypt are verily to be praised.

This response (based on Deut. 6:21) implies that the Passover does not simply commemorate a triumph of remote antiquity. Rather the Passover ceremony is a celebration of the emancipation of each Jew in every generation, for had it not been for the Exodus Jews would still be slaves in Egypt.

The keynote of the *Haggadah* is enshrined in a central pledge of the *seder*:

> It is the divine pledge that hath stood by our fathers and by us also. Not only one man has risen against us to destroy us, but in every generation men have risen against us to destroy us: But the Holy One delivereth us always from their hand.

Here Pharaoh's action is seen as a paradigm of all attempts by Israel's enemies to persecute the Jewish people. Echoes of centuries of persecution are evoked by these words, yet it is made clear that God has been, and will continue to be on the side of the oppressed people. In the symbols of the Passover meal, deliverance is re-enacted. Explaining this symbolism the leader states with regard to the shank-bone of the lamb:

> The Passover Lamb that our fathers used to eat when the Temple was still standing – that was because the Holy One, Blessed be He, passed over the house of our fathers in Egypt, as it is said: 'Ye shall say, It is the sacrifice of the Lord's Passover, who passed over the houses of children of Israel in Egypt, when He smote the Egyptians and delivered our houses.' And the people bowed the head and worshipped.

The unleavened bread is the bread of affliction, the historical emblem of the Exodus. The leader declares that it is the symbol of sympathy for the enslaved as well as that of freedom from oppression:

> This unleavened bread that we eat – what is the reason? It is because there was no time for our ancestors' dough to become leavened, before the King, King of all Kings, the Holy One, revealed Himself to them and redeemed them, as it is said: 'And they baked unleavened cakes of the dough which they brought forth out of Egypt, for it was not leavened: because they were thrust out of Egypt, and could not tarry, neither had they prepared for themselves any victual.'

The bitter herbs, the symbol of bitterness and servitude, remind the Jews that it is their duty as descendants of slaves to lighten the stranger's burden:

> This bitter herb that we eat – what is its reason? It is because the Egyptians embittered the life of our ancestors in Egypt, as it is said: 'And they made their lives bitter with hard bondage, in mortar and brick, and in all manner of service in the field, all their service, when they made them serve, was with rigour.'

The lesson of the Passover service – deeply engraved on the hearts of the Jewish nation – is that persecution and divine deliverance are realities of the present as well as the past. In each generation, Jews must think of themselves as delivered from a perpetual enemy and should assume the responsibility of rescuing those who suffer under oppression. The *Haggadah* states:

> In each and every generation it is a man's duty to regard himself as though he went forth out of Egypt, as it is said, 'And thou shalt tell thy son in that day saying, This is done because of that which the Lord did unto me when I came forth out of Egypt.' Not our fathers only did the Holy One redeem, but us too He redeemed, as it is said, 'And He brought us out from thence, that He might bring us in, to give us the Land which He swore unto our fathers.'

The Passover celebration is thus a symbolic exaltation of freedom; Jews are all to rejoice in God's liberation of their ancestors in which each of them takes part. Throughout the history of the Jewish people this festival has awakened the spirit of the people to the significance of human liberation. The biblical account of the Exodus, embodied in the liturgy of the *Haggadah*, has played a central role in the Jewish quest for human dignity and freedom. When we turn to the Passover in post-biblical literature, we find that Jewish writers also saw in the Exodus a source of hope and inspiration, even during the darkest hours of Jewish history. The lessons of the *Haggadah* were taught repeatedly by Jewish sages through commentary, interpretation and legend.

Reflecting on the significance of Passover, it is clear that Jews, like liberation theologians, have found renewed strength and hope in the message of the Exodus. The Passover ceremony unites the Jewish people with their ancestors who endured slavery and oppression in Egyptian bondage. Despite the persecution of centuries, the Jewish nation is confident of eventual deliverance and the ultimate redemption of humankind. The message of the Exodus calls the Jewish people to hold steadfast to their conviction that justice and freedom will prevail through the world. Thus Jews and Christian liberationists share a common biblical heritage and vision of the transformation of society, and the Exodus event unites them in a common hope and aspiration for the triumph of justice. Remembering the divine deliverance of the ancient Israelites, they can work together for the emancipation of all who are enslaved.

Christian Praxis

In *On Earth as it is in Heaven* I noted that the Exodus is understood by liberation theologians as the central salvific event in the history of ancient Israel. The reign of Pharaoh was oppressive; in response God chose to create a nation of free human beings. The Bible is hence a record of divine intervention in human history. What is required of Israel is obedient participation in the fulfilment of God's plan of emancipation. The faith of Israel is therefore portrayed as synonymous with acting in consonance with God's will. For liberation theologians the biblical witness leads to a historical orientation of the Christian faith. Praxis, rather than theological conceptualization, serves as the foundation of Christian commitment and obedience.

> Over against a theology of the word or of abstract principles, Latin America now posits a theology of lived faith, or committed action. Here a complete shift has taken place, and faith is understood as ortho-praxis rather than as orthodoxy (Pérez-Esclarín, 1978, 109).

For liberation theologians authentic theology must start from actions committed to the cause of the liberation. In this service theology is a praxis of liberation. Within this context Míguez Bonino stresses that Christianity must concern itself with modern society.

> We are not concerned with establishing through deduction the consequences of conceptual truths but with analysing a historical praxis which claims to be Christian. This critical analysis includes a number of operations which are totally unknown to classical theology. Historical praxis overflows beyond the area of the subjective and private. If we are dealing with acts and not merely with ideas, feelings, or intentions, we plunge immediately into the area of politics. (Míguez Bonino, 1975, 93).

Theology is here conceived as a critical reflection on praxis. In this context charity is given a central place in the Christian life; it is understood as the motivating force, the giving of oneself to others. In this light, Gutiérrez remarks, 'the understanding of faith appears as the understanding not of the simple affirmation – almost memorization – of truths, but of a commitment, an overall attitude, a particular posture toward life' (Gutiérrez, 1973, 7).

Similarly, Christian spirituality has undergone a major transformation. In the early centuries of the Church, contemplative life was characterized by withdrawal from the world. Today, however, liberation theologians emphasize that religion must engage actively in modern life.

> The revitalization of the religious life is come by way of our option for the poor classes on our continent. It is there that the following of Christ will find its embodiment in real history. If a people is capable of overcoming exploitation and building a fraternal society, in that very process it will be creating new forms of consecration to Christ and fidelity to our baptism. (Cussianovich, 1979, 164).

Christian action thus conceived must extend beyond the boundaries of the Church. Instead of using revelation and tradition as starting points – as in the past – Christian reflection must begin with facts and questions derived from history and the world. As Gutiérrez notes, it is precisely this openness to the totality of human history that allows theology to fulfil its critical function vis-à-vis ecclesiastical praxis (Gutiérrez, 1973, 12). Theology linked with praxis fulfils a prophetic function in so far as it interprets historical events in the light of God's purpose for humankind. The aim of such a theology is to make the Christian commitment clear and meaningful. Only in this fashion can the theologian engage in historical reality:

> He will be engaged where nations, social classes, people struggle to free themselves from domination and oppression by other nations, classes and people. In the last analysis, the true interpretation of the meaning revealed by theology is achieved only in historical praxis (Gutiérrez, 1973, 13).

In rendering an account of historical reality, liberation theologians have appealed to the social sciences to provide a basis for their view of society. In the past Christians used various philosophical systems to elaborate their views of God and humanity; for this reason liberationists feel fully justified in appropriating certain features of Marxist thought. Marxism, they believe, is an instrument of social analysis. By using the Marxist framework, liberation theologians find themselves better able to understand the world.

The interpretive context reveals that society is in a state of conflict in which major forces are polarized, unable to work together: the oppressors and the oppressed. Those who are exploited are not in control of their destiny; they are economically, politically and culturally dependent on others. Class struggle is thus a fact of life; to deny its reality is to side with the oppressors.

> When the Church rejects the class struggle, it is objectively operating as a part of the prevailing system. By denying the existence of social division, this system seeks to perpetuate this division on which are based the privileges of its beneficiaries (Gutiérrez, 1973, 275).

In such situations, one must inevitably take sides. Not to do so is in fact a decision to side with those in power; neutrality is impossible. In the past Christians tended to interpret evil in individualistic terms. Liberation theologians however insist that a society must itself change if evil is to be eliminated. For this reason, social and political action are central to the Church's message. A Marxist perspective provides a basis for understanding the nature of class conflict. For liberation theologians the struggle against oppression is seen as necessary and critical. The outcome of this conflict is not a new oppression, but the suppression of oppression and the elimination of evil. Míguez Bonino explains:

> Class struggle is not seen as a permanent fate of human existence and history but as an evil, triggered by the oppressive character of the present economic (social and political)

system; an evil that we must try to overcome by the elimination of this system (Míguez Bonino, 1975, 107).

The quest for a more human understanding of work is linked to class struggle. According to Marxism, workers in capitalist society are estranged from their work; labour is simply a purchased commodity. The response of many Christian liberation theologians is to protest against this dehumanized conception of human toil. What is needed instead is for labourers to realize themselves in their work. This can only be done, liberationists insist, by changing the structure of production, by replacing capitalism with socialism.

According to some liberation theologians, such a transformation of society can take place only through violent revolution. The theory of revolution is based on an analysis of the structures of injustice and oppression. Inevitably those who possess wealth and power will resist change. 'So we are presented,' Ellacuría writes, 'with the necessity of exerting force against the unjust will of those who hold power in the oppressive structural set up which crucifies the weak' (Ellacuriá, 1976, 209). Violence is therefore legitimate if it is used to redeem the enslaved. In this context the struggle against violence should not be regarded as violence; instead it should be seen as a force that is necessary to redeem the established violence against humankind.

The belief in a Utopian vision of the future to be created through human action is far removed from traditional Christian eschatology. The hope of the Kingdom to come worked against social and political activity; liberation theologians, however, aim to change the world, and their writings are intended to galvanize others into action. In transferring Christian thought, these Christian writers look to their Jewish heritage for models of divine activity. In the Exodus narrative in particular they discover the essential elements of theology in which divine will and human response are found together. Thus the Jewish Scriptures serve as the starting point for a theology of liberation in which:

God's action takes place in history and as history. It inextricably involves human action and, conversely, there is no human action reported outside the relation with God's purpose and world . . . Yahweh's sovereignty does not appear in history as an abstract act or an interpretation but as announcement and commandment, as an announcement which convokes, as promise and judgment, demanding and inviting a response (Míguez Bonino, 1975, 134).

Jewish Ortho-praxis

In my presentation in *On Earth as it is in Heaven* I stressed that through the centuries Judaism did not separate religion from life; instead Jews were called to action, to turn humankind away from violence, wickedness, and falsehood. It was not the hope of bliss in a future life but the establishment of the Kingdom of justice and peace that is central to the Jewish faith. Moral praxis is at the heart of the religious tradition. The people of Israel as a light to the nations reflects the moral nature of God; each Jew is to be like the Creator, mirroring the divine qualities revealed to Moses: 'The Lord, the Lord, a God merciful and gracious, slow to anger, and abounding in steadfast love and faithfulness keeping steadfast love for thousands, forgiving iniquity and transgression and sin' (Exod. 34:6–7).

God as a moral being demands moral living, as the Psalms declare: 'The Lord is righteous; He loves righteous deeds' (Ps 11:7). 'Righteousness and justice are the foundation of His throne' (Ps 97:2). 'Thou has established equity; thou hast executed justice and righteousness (Ps 99:4). Given this theological framework, Jews are directed to obey the revealed will of God, which was the basis of the covenantal relationship between God and the Jewish nation. Orthopraxis, rather than conceptual reflection, serves as the foundation of the religion of Israel.

In the Bible, deeds and events involving moral issues

are found in abundance: the punishment of Cain for murdering his brother, the violence of the generation that brought on the Flood, the early prohibition against murder, the hospitality of Abraham and his pleading for the people of Sodom, the praise of Abraham for his moral attitudes, the condemnation of Joseph's brothers, Joseph's self-restraint in the house of Potiphar, Moses' intercessions on the side of the exploited (Spero, 1983, 22).

But it is pre-eminently in the legal codes of the Pentateuch that we encounter moral guidelines formulated in specific rules. The Decalogue in particular illustrates the centrality of moral praxis in the life of the Jew. The first four commandments are theological in character, but the last six deal with relationships between human beings. The first commandment describes God as the one who redeemed the Jews from Egypt; the one who forbade the worship of other deities and demands respect for the Sabbath and the divine name. These commandments are expressions of the love and fear of God; the remaining injunctions provide a means of expressing love of other human beings. The Decalogue makes it clear that moral rules are fundamental to the Jewish faith.

Such ethical standards are repeated in the prophetic books. The teachings of the prophets are rooted in the Torah of Moses. The prophets saw themselves as messengers of the divine word; their special task was to denounce the people for their transgressions and call them to repentance. In all this they pointed to concrete action – moral praxis – as the only means of sustaining the covenantal relationship with God. The essential theme of their message is that God demands righteousness and justice. Here, as in the rest of the Bible, the moral life is seen as the foundation of the Jewish faith. Theology is defined in relation to practical activity; it is through ethical praxis that humanity encounters the divine.

Rabbinic literature continues this emphasis on action. Convinced they were the authentic expositors of Scripture, the rabbis amplified biblical law. In their presentation of the commandments, rabbinic exegetes differentiate between the laws governing human relationships to God and those that concern human relationships to others. As in the biblical period, rabbinic teachings reflect the same sense of the primacy of morality. Thus, in the classic texts of Judaism, moral behaviour is the predominant theme. By choosing the moral life, the Jew can help to complete God's work of creation. To accomplish this task the rabbis formulated an elaborate system of traditions, which were written down in the Mishnah, subsequently expanded in the Talmud, and eventually codified in the Code of Jewish Law. In all cases the law is precise and specific; it is God's word made concrete in the daily life of the Jew.

In contrast to this emphasis on the centrality of moral praxis, the Jewish religion does not insist on the acceptance of formal theological dogma. Like liberation theology, the hallmark of the Jewish tradition is ortho-praxis rather than theological orthodoxy. In the history of the Jewish faith there has never been a central body that took upon itself the responsibility of formulating a religious creed. The books of the Bible and early rabbinic literature contain numerous beliefs about God's nature and activity, yet neither the Bible, the Mishnah, nor the Talmud contain a list of correct beliefs. Only infrequently in the development of early rabbinic Judaism were there attempts to categorize the essential principles of Judaism. It was not until the Middle Ages – when Jewish scholars faced the challenge of Greek philosophical thought as well as Christianity and Islam – did they feel it necessary to outline the essential theological features of their faith. But even then Jewish thinkers were unable to reach unanimous agreement. Thus within the mainstream Judaism there is great scope for individual interpretation. The theological views of individual teachers are their own opinions, enjoying only as much authority as the teachers' learning. All Jews are obligated to accept the divine origin of the Law, but this is not so with regard to the various theological concepts expounded by the rabbis.

We can see therefore that the Jewish tradition places halachic observance at its centre. Though the Jewish faith is based on the belief of God's action in history and revelation of the Torah, individual theological speculation is not regarded as authoritative. The Law, as contained in the Pentateuch and expanded by the rabbis is the basis of the religious system. As with liberation theology, action – in particular moral praxis – is at the heart of the faith. Of primary importance is the translation of religious conviction into concrete behaviour in this world. God's truth is to be fulfilled by deeds of loving-kindness; according to both traditions, faith is the total human response to God. True faith is not a simple affirmation of abstract truths as formulated in a creed, but a commitment, an overall attitude, a particular posture to life. Faith in action – ethical praxis – is the truest expression of religious devotion, and in this both Judaism and liberation theology stand together in the quest for a better world.

Common Ground

In *On Earth as it is in Heaven* I insisted that despite the overlap between Christian liberation theology and Jewish thought, there are important theological differences. As in the past, Jews today would regard the liberationist's adherence to traditional Christology as misguided. For the Jew, God is an absolute unity; He is indivisible and unique, containing no plurality. Given this understanding, the doctrine of the Incarnation must be rejected. The belief that Jesus was both man and God continues to be considered a blasphemous heresy. Contemporary Jewish thinkers also reject trinitarianism in any form; there is simply no way to harmonize the belief in Jewish monotheism with the conception of a triune God. Similarly, Jews of all degrees of observance deny the liberationist's claim that Jesus is the Messiah. For Jews, Jesus did not fulfil the messianic expectations: he did not gather in the exiles and restore the Law; he did not rebuild the Temple; nor did he bring about a cataclysmic change in human history. Further, Jews deny that Jesus had an extraordinary relationship with God and that he can forgive sins.

None the less Jews can find much to sympathize with in liberation theology. As we have seen, liberationists focus on the flesh-and-blood Jesus of the gospels; they have reclaimed the historical context of the New Testament. Instead of analysing Jesus' divine and human character, the facts of the ministry of Jesus provide the basis for their theology. Like the prophets of the Old Testament, Jesus is seen as the conscience of Israel. Just as the ancient prophets criticized the people of Israel for their iniquity so did Jesus attack the scribes and Pharisees for their lack of righteousness. Given this understanding, it is possible for Jews to gain an appreciation of Jesus' mission.

Jesus' departure from Jewish Law should therefore not be construed as a rejection of Judaism itself, but as a critique of religious corruption and moral stagnation. In his confrontations with the leaders of the nation, Jesus echoed the words of the prophets by denouncing hypocrisy and injustice. The love of wealth and the exploitation of the poor, he contended, made it impossible to establish a proper relationship with God. It was his conviction that the leaders had led the people away from true worship of God; in his ministry Jesus opposed a life of ritual practice devoid of moral concern. As a prophetic figure Jesus should be recognizable to all Jews; like the prophets, he emphasized that loving-kindness is at the heart of the Jewish faith. Jesus' words thus recalled such figures as Amos, Hosea, Isaiah, and Jeremiah; he stood firmly within the Jewish tradition.

By concentrating on Jesus' prophetic role and ministry, liberation theologians have brought the temporal dimension into prominence. Putting into the background Christianity's otherwordly outlook, they stress that Christian action is of primary concern. The Kingdom of God, they state, must be understood as intimately connected with the establishment of justice. As in Judaism, the Kingdom is conceived by liberation theologians as taking place on the terrestrial plane. Jesus inaugurated the first stage of this process – the building of God's Kingdom, which entails a total transformation of the old order through active struggle. By declaring the coming of the Kingdom, Jesus was issuing a call to strive for the physical and spiritual liberation of the oppressed. Social structures must be changed if peace and justice are to be established. Such an understanding of Jesus' message is an important departure from traditional Christian thought; the emphasis on social realities rather than internal attitudes is a profound shift from the past.

This radical break with previous Christian concepts of the Kingdom is of vital significance for the Jewish perception of liberation theology. Though Jews are unable to accept the claim that Jesus ushered in the period of messianic redemption, they can easily accept the liberationists' view that God wants everyone to take part in bringing about the Kingdom of God. As we have seen, this understanding is a fundamental element of the theology of the Hebrew Scriptures as well as of rabbinic thought; for the Jews the Kingdom of God consists of a complete moral order. The fulfilment of this conception ultimately rests with the Messiah, but it is humanity's duty to participate in the creation of a better society in anticipation of the messianic redemption. Throughout Jewish literature, Jews have been called to bring about the rule of truth and holiness. Thus for both Jews and liberation theologians the establishment of the Kingdom of God is a process in which all human beings have an important role. The rejection of an internalized, spiritual, and otherworldly Kingdom draws liberation theology back to its Jewish roots.

In this struggle to bring about God's Kingdom, liberation theologians constantly look back to the history of the Jewish people for inspiration. Nowhere is this more apparent than in their use of the Exodus experience as a paradigm of liberation. In their exposition of the biblical account, liberationists emphasize that God was on the side of the afflicted. The Exodus event is of equal significance for the Jewish nation; for the Jews God is the Saviour of the people. The Exodus experience is a core event in the self-understanding of the Jews. In Jewish sources and in the Passover liturgy, the deliverance from Egypt is seen as a symbol of freedom. Throughout the Passover meal Jews are admonished to remember that they were slaves in Egypt so that they will take sides with those persecuted today. Passover is not simply a festival commemorating a past occurrence. It is a perpetual reminder that human emancipation must take place everywhere. Jews and liberationists thus share a common heritage and vision of a future in which all humankind will be delivered from bondage.

In the account of the Exodus from Egypt, the faith of Israel was portrayed as a response to God's will. What is required of Israel is obedient participation in the act of emancipation. For liberation theologians this biblical anchorage leads to a practical orientation of the faith: praxis, rather than theological reflection, is understood as the key to Christian witness. Liberation theologians stress that theology must start from actions committed to the process of liberation; theology is a critical reflection on praxis.

For Jews the emphasis on the concrete dimension of faith is essential. The Jewish hope lies in God's rule on earth. This is the goal of the history of the world in which the Jewish people have a central role. Throughout the Bible and in rabbinic literature ethical behaviour is the predominant theme. By doing God's will the Jew can help complete the work of creation. As in liberation theology, the Jewish religion focuses on orthopraxis rather than theological orthodoxy. Theological speculation is not seen as authoritative; instead moral praxis is at the core of the faith. Deeds of goodness rather than dogma take precedence. Jewish and Christian liberation theologians are thus united in the quest for the total elimination of human wickedness.

This shared vision can serve as a bridge between the two traditions. Liberation theology's return to traditional Jewish ideals should make it possible for both faiths to work together for the first time in areas of social concern. Liberation theologians have paved the way for such a common endeavour by explaining how ethical values rooted in the Bible can be put into practice. In pursuit of the common goal of freedom from oppression, committed Jews and Christians can become a saving remnant in the modern world, embodying the liberation message of Scripture. Like Abraham they can hope against hope in labouring to build a more just and humane world. They can become an Abrahamic minority, attentive to the cry of oppression.

We are told that Abraham and other partiarchs heard the voice of God. Can we also hear the Lord's call? We live in a world where millions of our fellow men live in inhuman conditions, practically in slavery. If we are not deaf, we hear the cries of the oppressed. Their cries are the voice of God. We who live in rich countries where there are always pockets of underdevelopment and wretchedness, hear if we want to hear, the unvoiced demands of those who have no voice and no hope. The pleas of those who have no voice and no hope are the voice of God (Camara, 1976, 16).

2 Liberation Theology in a Post-Holocaust World

On Earth as it is in Heaven: Jews, Christians and Liberation Theology was a first step in establishing connections between Christian liberation theology and the Jewish heritage. In the same year (1987) another book on this topic by Marc Ellis was published by Orbis: *Toward a Jewish Theology of Liberation*. Although not as theologically orientated as *On Earth as it is in Heaven*, this work also focuses on the contribution of liberation theology to a recovery of prophetic ideals. However Ellis's study concentrates on the implications of political empowerment in modern society. According to Ellis, in Israel and within the American Jewish community policies and alliances have emerged which resemble those previously used to oppress Jewry. For Ellis, the drive into southern Lebanon and the subjugation of Palestinians of the West Bank and Gaza are a betrayal of the Jewish tradition. Similarly he regards the exploitation of the poor in the United States, as well as American efforts to establish Israel as a US outpost, as undermining the ethical demands of Judaism. These developments, he maintains, threaten the integrity and future of the Jewish people; none the less Christian liberation theology can awaken contemporary Jewry from its moral slumber and encourage Jews to remain loyal to their prophetic inheritance.

The Challenge of the Holocaust

In contemporary society the death of millions of Jews in the concentration camps has overwhelmed the Jewish community. In *Toward a Jewish Theology of Liberation*, Ellis points to the significance of this event. The numerous accounts of this tragedy illustrate the Nazi intention to rid the world of the Jewish people. The testimonies of survivors of the camps bear witness to the sense of desolation of these victims as well as their desire for death. Thus a Jewess who miraculously survived being shot and buried in a mass grave recalled:

> And yet with my last strength I came up on the top of the grave, and when I did, I did not know the place, so many bodies were lying all over, dead people; I wanted to see the end of this stretch of dead bodies but I could not. It was impossible. They were lying all over, all dying; suffering; naked; shot, but not dead . . . I was praying, for the grave to be opened and to swallow me alive. Blood was spurting from the grave in many places, like a well of water, I dug with my fingernails, but the grave would not open, I did not have enough strength. I cried out to my mother, to my father, 'Why did they not kill me? What was my sin? I have no one to go to.' (Israel v. Adolph Eichmann, pp. L1, M1, M2, N1).

What sense can be made of such horror? For many survivors, their sense of abandonment was overwhelming. In the words of Alexander Donat, an inmate of Treblinka:

> In vain we looked at that cloudless September sky for some sign of God's wrath. The heavens were silent. In vain we waited to hear from the lips of the great ones of the world, the champions of light and justice . . . In vain we implored help from our Polish brothers with whom we had shared good and bad alike for seven centuries, but they were utterly unmoved in our hour of anguish (Ellis, 1987, 10).

In the decades following this tragedy, a number of Jewish thinkers have struggled to come to terms with the Shoah. In his book Ellis cites the work of two major figures. The first, Elie Wiesel, has explored the religious implications of the Holocaust in a series of novels and essays. As a young boy he experienced the shattering of his faith after arriving at Auschwitz.

Never shall I forget that night, the first night in camp which has turned my life into one long night, seven times cursed and seven times sealed. Never shall I forget that smoke. Never shall I forget the little faces of children, whose bodies I saw turned into wreaths of smoke beneath a silent blue sky. Never shall I forget those flames which consumed my faith forever. Never shall I forget that nocturnal silence which deprived me for all eternity of the desire to live. Never shall I forget those moments which murdered my God and my soul and turned my dreams to dust (Wiesel, 1969, 44).

Such rebellion intensified during his imprisonment. At Rosh Hashanah (the New Year), he recoiled from blessing God as he heard the inmates of the camp repeat the prayer: 'Blessed be the Name of the Eternal.'

Why, but why should I bless Him? In every fibre I rebelled. Because He had had thousands of children burned in His pits? Because He kept six crematories working night and day, on Sundays and feast days. Because in His great might He had created Auschwitz, Birkenau, Buna, and so many factories of death? How could I say to Him: 'Blessed art Thou, Eternal, Master of the Universe, Who chose us from among the races to be tortured day and night, to see our fathers, our mothers, our brothers, end in the crematory? Praised by Thy Holy Name, Thou Who hast chosen us to be butchered on Thine altar?' (Wiesel, 1969, 78).

Later, when two Jewish adults and one child were hanged, someone asked: 'Where is God? Where is He?' Viewing this terrible spectacle, Wiesel recalled:

The two adults were no longer alive. Their tongues hung swollen, blue-tinged. But the third rope was still moving; being so light, the child was still alive . . . For more than half an hour he stayed there, struggling between life and death, dying a slow agony under our eyes. And we had to look him full in the face. He was still alive when I passed in front of him. His tongue was still red, his eyes not yet glazed. Behind me, I heard the same man asking: 'Where is God now?' And I heard a voice within me answer him: 'Where is He? Here He is – He is hanging here on this gallows' (Wiesel, 1969, 76).

Wiesel's protest against God's seeming indifference is mirrored in the writings of the radical theologian Richard Rubenstein. For Rubenstein, the Holocaust calls into question the existence of an omnipotent, benevolent God of history. In *After Auschwitz* Rubenstein argues that it is impossible to sustain a belief in a supernatural deity after the events of the Nazi era. Traditional Jewish theology maintains that God is the ultimate actor in history – it interprets every tragedy as God's punishment for Israel's sinfulness. But Rubenstein is unable to see how this position can be maintained without viewing Hitler as an instrument of His will:

> The agony of European Jewry cannot be likened to the testing of Job. To see any purpose in the death camps, the traditional believer is forced to regard the most demonic, anti-human explosion of all history as a meaningful expression of God's purposes. The idea is simply too obscene for me to accept (Rubenstein, 1966).

According to Rubenstein a void now exists where once the Jewish people experienced God's presence. This demythologizing of the Jewish tradition is, he argues, acknowledged in contemporary Jewish life even if it is not made explicit in Jewish theology. In the diaspora and in Israel the myth of an omnipotent God of history is effectively repudiated in the lives of most Jewish people. After the Nazi period, life is lived and enjoyed on its own terms without any superordinant values or special theological relationship. According to Rubenstein, we live in the time of the death of God. He is compelled to use such terminology because it conveys the contemporary Jewish experience of God's absence:

> When I say we live in the time of the death of God I mean that the thread uniting God and man, heaven and earth, has been broken. We stand in a cold, silent, unfeeling cosmos, unaided by any powerful power beyond our own resources. After Auschwitz, what else can a Jew say about God? (as quoted in Cohn-Sherbok, 1989, 82).

Beyond Despair

Such reactions to the terrors of the Nazi era point to a profound theological crisis. Yet there are a number of contemporary Jewish thinkers who have provided a much more positive response. Here Ellis cites the work of the Jewish theologian Emil Fackenheim. In *God's Presence in History: Jewish Affirmations and Philosophical Reflections*, Fackenheim gives a full explanation of his point of view.

For Fackenheim, it is a sacred duty to remember the Holocaust. The intention of the Nazis was to eliminate all Jews – no survivor was to be left the tell the story of the horrors that took place. They were making as sure as possible that every trace of memory was wiped out. Millions would be as though they had never been. The Commanding Voice of Auschwitz demands that those who perished must never be forgotten. It is a holy duty to remember and tell the tale – such an obligation is not negotiable.

Fackenheim insists that the Holocaust must continue to be resisted in contemporary society. Civilization now includes the death camps and those who understand what took place in the Holocaust cannot overlook the rationally organized, systematic, excremental assault on the Jewish people. As a consequence, resistance to the Holocaust and the quest for *tikkun* (cosmic repair) have become never-ending imperatives. Further, Fackenheim stresses that only as a result of the deed of resistance can resisting thought be effective. In the case of those inmates who had the courage to act, thought and action were united. Their acknowledgement of the Nazi logic of destruction helped produce resistance to it. Just as the Holocaust was a *novum* in history, so too this resistance was a *novum* – it was a way of being and a way of thought. Fackenheim cites the testimony of Pelagia Lewinska, a Polish Catholic, who illuminatingly represents such a combination of thought and deed:

At the outset the living places, the ditches, the mud, the piles of excrement behind the blocks, had appalled me with their horrific filth . . . and then I saw the light! I saw that it was not a question of disorder or lack of organization but that, on the contrary, a very thoroughly considered conscious idea was in the back of the camp's existence. They had condemned us to die in our own filth, to drown in mud, in our own excrement. They wished to abase us, to destroy our human dignity, to efface every vestige of humanity . . . to fill us with horror and contempt towards ourselves and our fellows . . . From the instant when I grasped the motivating principle . . . it was as if I had been awakened from a dream . . . I felt under orders to live . . . And if I did die in Auschwitz, it would be as a human being, I would hold on to my dignity (Fackenheim, 1982, 25–6).

For Fackenheim such commitment is of central importance. Lewinska felt obliged to resist and endure – her experience is evidence of God's Commanding Voice. Responding to this same divine call, the Jewish community must become a witness to the world of survival and perseverance in a post-Holocaust age.

In various writings, another major Jewish theologian Irving Greenberg confronts the implications of the Holocaust for modernity. According to Greenberg the destruction of six million Jews is an indictment of the twentieth century as well as of Judaism and Christianity. Both contemporary society and religion have passed over the challenge of the Holocaust in silence. The message of the victims (to stop the massacre of the innocent and re-evaluate social and religious life) has been ignored. In Greenberg's view, for the past two centuries the Lord of history and revelation has been supplanted by the 'Lord of Science and Humanism'. Yet the horrors of the camps cause one to question whether such a substitution makes sense. For Greenberg those who died at the hands of Nazis ask above anything else not to allow the creation of another set of values that might sustain another attempt at genocide.

Greenberg asserts that after Auschwitz, it is possible to speak only of 'moment faiths', namely instances when a vision of redemption is infused with the flames and smoke of burning children. Such 'moment faiths' constitute the end of the distinction between atheist and theist and the equation of faith with doctrine. In the aftermath of the Shoah, the difference between the sceptic and the devout resides in the frequency of faith rather than in certitude. This dialectic is illustrated by the creation of a Jewish State:

> If Treblinka makes human hope an illusion, then the Western Wall asserts that human dreams are more real than force and facts. Israel's faith in the God of History demands that an unprecedented event of destruction be matched by an unprecedented act of redemption, and this has happened (Greenberg, 1977, 29).

In a post-Holocaust world, it is imperative that the Jewish community refuse to victimize others:

> The Holocaust cannot be used for triumphalism. Its moral challenge must also be applied to Jews. Those Jews who feel no guilt for the Holocaust are also tempted to moral apathy. Religious Jews who use the Holocaust to morally impugn every other religious group but their own are the ones who are tempted thereby into indifference at the Holocaust of others. Those Israelis who place as much distance as possible between the weak, passive Diaspora victims and the 'mighty Sabras' are tempted to use Israeli strength indiscriminately (i.e. beyond what is absolutely inescapable for self-defence and survival), which is to risk turning other people into victims of the Jews. Neither faith nor morality can function without serious twisting of perspective, even to the point of becoming demonic, unless they are illuminated by the fires of Auschwitz and Treblinka (Greenberg, 1977, 22).

Jewish Empowerment and Ethical Values

Those thinkers who have grappled with the religious perplexities of the Holocaust have focused on the significance of the creation of the Jewish State. In different ways they see this event as central to Jewish survival in the modern world. By establishing a homeland in Israel the Jewish people has expressed its commitment to the future of Judaism – political empowerment is thus an expression of fidelity to those who died in the concentration camps. Yet, according to Ellis, such a solution to Jewish existence poses a central dilemma: the desire to nurture life is often frustrated by the demands of national security. Further, the entry into history can lead to an abuse of power:

> Having emerged from the prospect of annihilation, the Jewish community thus has entered a present that offers both fruitful possibility and danger. The formative event of the Holocaust can serve to legitimate or critique power; what we do with that event will determine how the desire to be faithful works itself out concretely in history (Ellis, 1987, 23).

Since Jews were victimized in the past, Ellis states, they should feel commitment to those who are presently undergoing hardship and suffering. Yet political empowerment has tended to blunt the sensitivity of the nation. In their liberation, the meaning of slavery is in danger of being lost. In expounding this view Ellis refers to the work of Irving Greenberg, who in his writings grapples with the realities of the Holocaust and empowerment. For Greenberg Jewish history can be divided into three epochs: biblical, rabbinic and modern. During the biblical period the nation struggled to harmonize convenantal values with political sovereignty. When the leaders of the nation failed to uphold Jewish values the prophets condemned the nation for its unrighteousness. The biblical era was also marked by God's frequent intervention on behalf of His chosen people. But with the destruction of the second Temple in AD 70, a crisis of faith occurred. How could God have allowed this event to take place? Had he rejected the Jewish nation and allowed it to be devastated? In response to this dilemma, the rabbis emphasized the importance of Torah study. In this way Jewry was able to compensate for the loss of the Temple and its national sovereignty. According to Greenberg, the rabbis engaged in a central theological revision: as divine presence and activity diminished in the life of the nation, the convenant was renewed. Thus God called the people to a new stage of service.

By interpreting Jewish history in this way, the sages were able to assure the nation that the divine covenant had not been broken. In essence they created a new meaning to Jewish history through the reinterpretation of powerlessness and exile. This was the hallmark of the second era of Jewish existence. The next epoch began with the Holocaust and the ensuing collapse of religious commitment. In this third stage of Jewish history the people are called to testify to a new degree of covenantal responsibility:

> If God did not stop the murder and the torture, then what was the statement made by the infinitely suffering Divine Presence in Auschwitz? It was a cry for action, a call to humans to stop the Holocaust, a call to the people of Israel to rise to a new, unprecedented level of covenantal responsibility. It was as if God said: 'Enough, stop it, never again, bring redemption!' The world did not heed that call and stop the Holocaust. European Jews were unable to respond. World Jewry did not respond adequately. But the response finally did come with the creation of the State of Israel. The Jews took on enough power and responsibility to act. And this call was answered as much by so-called secular Jews as by the so-called religious. Even as God was in Treblinka, so God went up with Israel to Jerusalem (Greenberg, 1977, 18).

This change from powerlessness to political empowerment is inescapable in the face of the Holocaust. No longer is it possible for Jews to remain dependent on the goodwill of other nations. However, Greenberg is aware that political empowerment will test the ability of the tradition to advance principles consonant with the Jewish tradition. In the third era pragmatism rather than a prophetic vision will animate the nation. This shift to pragmatism and compromise symbolizes the end of utopian ideals and sanctions the occasional use of immoral strategies to achieve moral ends.

The tension between *Realpolitik* and idealism is found predominantly in Israel. Although Greenberg believes that it is incumbent on the Jewish nation to allow as much self-government for Palestinians and Arabs as possible, this can only be accepted if it does not pose a threat to Jewish security.

> To yield autonomy without overwhelming proof of Palestinian desire to live in peace is to invite martyrdom and morally reprehensible death by genocide. The Palestinians will have to earn their power by living peacefully and convincing Israel of their beneficence or by acquiescing to a situation in which Israel's strength guarantees that the Arabs cannot use their power to endanger Israel (Greenberg, 1977, 26).

Although Ellis agrees with Greenberg's portrayal of contemporary Jewish values, he is anxious to point out that Greenberg fails to acknowledge the centrality of the prophetic aspects of the Torah tradition:

> The ability to understand another's story and hear another's pain, to recognize the formation of other peoples and their struggle for freedom to be as important as our own and as a legitimate demand upon us – this seems to be non-existent in Greenberg's analysis (Ellis, 1987, 36).

Greenberg contends that power is now necessary for survival in contemporary society. In Israel achieving power is a sacred principle – to endanger it is unforgivable. In the post-Holocaust era denying power is equivalent to the excommunicable sins of earlier ages. For Ellis this view of empowerment undermines the Jewish tradition. The insights of biblical and rabbinic Judaism are repressed in order to maintain the Jewish people's newly acquired national identity. Though Greenberg is progressive about social issues, his views provide a religious framework for neo-conservatism within the Jewish community. Empowerment almost without restraint has become the ideology of this movement. According to Ellis, Greenberg's analysis of the State of Israel as the answer to the Holocaust, as the redemption out of nothingness, can be used as a basis for actions which run counter to the spirit of Judaism. 'If it is true that a totally ethical people cannot survive,' Ellis writes, 'it is also true that we may be in danger of being a people void of ethics.' (Ellis, 1987, 36).

The Ethical Imperative

In expounding his thesis Ellis also refers to the writing of Nathan and Ruth Ann Perlmutter. In *The Real Anti-Semitism in America*, these writers argue that many non-Jews accept the anti-Semitic stereotypes of Jews, sentiments which are inimical to the Jewish people in the United States and Israel. In the United Nations, for example, Zionism has been equated with racism; in the 1980s a Jordanian delegate invoked the anti-semitic forgery *Protocols of the Elders of Zion* as evidence of a Jewish international conspiracy. According to the Perlmutters, such hatred of Jews if fuelled by today's revolutionary governments as well as by liberal groups in the United States. Black leadership in America, for instance, has become increasingly anti-Jewish in its attitudes and pronouncements. Similarly, liberal Protestant groups such as the National Council of Churches has made pronouncements detrimental to Israel.

In the light of the shift of allegiance, Jews need to form new alliances with those who are currently pro-Jewish. This means for example, a reversal of long-held Jewish views towards fundamentalists who are now among Israel's strongest allies. The view advanced by the Perlmutters has become the policy of many American Jewish institutions. Yet, for Ellis, such attitudes ignore the ethical dimensions of the Jewish faith. *Realpolitik*, he believes, should not be allowed to replace the ideals which have animated Jews throughout the ages:

> The Perlmutters' analysis is increasingly held by American Jews and is the one most available through media and from Jewish institutions such as the Anti-Defamation League of B'nai Brith, for whom Nathan Perlmutter works. It is in a sense a logical extension of Greenberg's theological works – one way of looking at the post-Holocaust world. However, there also exists an articulate and active minority that is critical of such views and seeks to reestablish the prophetic and ethical dimensions of the Jewish community (Ellis, 1987, 39).

Ellis continues this discussion of contemporary Jewish

values by considering the work of Earl Shorris, *Jews Without Mercy: A Lament*, and Roberta Strauss Feuerlicht, *The Fate of the Jews: A People Torn Between Israeli Power and Jewish Ethics*. For Shorris, Judaism is a religion based on ethical principles. Yet in the modern world the moral aspects of the Jewish faith have been superseded by a pragmatic approach to Jewish survival. According to this ideology, Jews should not help minority groups because they will inevitably be disloyal; Palestinians should not be granted a State since they pose a threat to Israel; any political position taken by American Jews is justified if it helps Israel. Shorris is incensed by such attitudes:

> The new definition of Jewish interests belongs to an arrogant people . . . How can it belong to a people who have been instructed to be a 'light to the nations'? The new definition belongs to a people of unlimited power and no history. How can it belong to a people who remember that they were 'sojourners in Egypt'? One can understand how Jews could fear the outside world or wish for a homeland or wish to disappear safely into another culture or seek the good life for all so that they might enjoy it as well. The new definition has the chill of loneliness about it. The expressions of it are sometimes grasping, sometimes combative, sometimes vengeful (Shorris, 1982, 60).

Shorris's analysis raises the question whether those who adopt such neo-conservatism have changed the definition of what it means to be Jewish.

Feuerlicht also assesses this shift from traditional Jewish ideals. Like Shorris, Feuerlicht believes that Judaism is based on moral standards:

> Whether Jews are a religion, a people, a civilization, a historical process or an anomaly, whether they are Hasidim or heretics, what binds all Jews from antiquity to the present is not statehood but the burden they placed upon themselves and posterity when they internalized morality and gave the world the ethical imperative (Feuerlicht, 1983, 5).

Nonetheless modern Jewry has betrayed this fundamental dimension of the Jewish heritage. This has occurred particularly with regard to the State of Israel. According to Feuerlicht, Israel was imposed upon the indigenous population by a non-resident power and this policy of exploitation and denial of Palestinian rights continues today in the occupied territories. Palestinians are dependent on Israeli corporations and the government through expropriation of their land, and they are discriminated against in areas of employment, education and land use. When Palestinians protest about such injustices, they are blacklisted, arrested and tortured.

For centuries Jews lived in exile – they were denied human rights and were subject to discrimination and persecution. Today Arabs are being treated in a similar fashion by Israelis. For Feuerlicht this reversal of roles is a violation of the Jewish tradition. Despite this critcism, Feuerlicht believes that the State of Israel must continue to exist, but it needs to change its course or it will be morally bankrupt. According to Ellis, Feuerlicht's analysis of modern Jewish life highlights the need for Jews to alter their priorities. In contemporary society the Jewish people have embraced new idols: capitalism, nationalism, and survival at any cost. What is required today is for Jewry to be sympathetic and supportive of those who are currently struggling for a liberation from oppression and exploitation. As Ellis writes, a critical exploration of contemporary Jewish attitudes may open 'a path of generosity toward other struggling communities and decrease our new-found arrogance and our consequent isolation from liberation movements around the globe' (Ellis, 1987, 46).

A New Jewish Vision

In the post-Holocaust world many Jews believe that Jewish survival depends on the existence of a Jewish State. Others, however, maintain that ethical values embedded within the Jewish tradition constitute the Jews' essential witness to all peoples. According to Ellis there are three contemporary movements for moral renewal within the Jewish community. The first group is composed of those who have recently become actively involved in Jewish life. A considerable number of these converts to Orthodoxy – known as Ba'alei Teshuvah – are from upper- and middle-class suburban communities, who in the 1960s and 1970s protested against the Vietnam War, racial conflict and consumerism. In Judaism these young people have found a source of spiritual strength. Some of those who have returned to Orthodox Judaism previously led active political lives on the left – they were animated by Jewish ethical concern without recognizing its origin. Through their discovery of the Jewish tradition, their political convictions have been deepened.

As an example of such transformation, Ellis cites the case of Arthur Waskow, who worked as a social activist and subsequently became committed to Orthodox Judaism. Ten days after the assassination of Martin Luther King, Waskow celebrated the Passover *seder*, an event which drew him back to Judaism. 'Tonight was the beginning of the Passover,' he wrote. 'It was the time for my encounter with the sacred past' (as quoted in Ellis, 1987, 49).

For Waskow, the Torah serves as a framework for living an authentic Jewish life. Torah discussion, particularly as found in *havurot* (small Jewish fellowship groups), can kindle a common process of religious growth. Today the Jewish people have created institutions with political influence – it is necessary to make certain they incorporate prophetic value. Further, Waskow argues that today the Torah should enable humankind to transform the world. In this regard he notes that the Jewish faith contains teachings different from what is contained in secular ideologies such as socialism, capitalism, nationalism and science. Waskow's return to Orthodoxy is an illustration of one of the most important sources for Jewish renewal in contemporary society.

Another movement for regeneration consists of those who address social and political issues without such a return to Orthodoxy. Such a group is the new Jewish Agenda which has brought progressive Jews together to counteract political and religious neo-conservatism. According to its statement of purpose:

> We are Jews from a variety of backgrounds and affiliations committed to progressive human values and the building of a shared vision of Jewish life . . . many of us find our inspiration in our people's historical resistance to oppression and from the Jewish presence at the forefront of movements for social change. Many of us base our convictions on the religious concept of *Tikkun Olam* (the just ordering of human society and the world) and the prophetic tradition of social justice (New Jewish Agenda National Platform, 28 Nov. 1982, p. 1).

The platform adopted by the New Jewish Agenda includes progressive positions on racism, lesbianism, gay rights and Israel.

In attempting to carry out their programme members of this organization are involved in a variety of concerns. For example, in 1984 this group organized the Jewish Human Rights Delegation to Nicaragua. In December of that year a delegation sponsored by the New Jewish Agenda arrived in Nicaragua and spent a week in various villages. In a statement read in front of the American Embassy they declared:

> Our Judaism brings us to this place because our tradition asks us to speak out against injustice. We, as a people, are dedicated to *Tikkun Olam*, the just restitution and repair of the world. Through our tradition, we have accepted that responsibility of preserving the world in our laws, our text and mostly, our hearts (as quoted in Ellis, 1987, 55).

In Israel another movement, *Oz VeShalom* (Religious Zionists for Strength and Peace), has been established in response to the misinterpretation of biblical texts and religious Zionism. In particular this group is critical of Jewish settlements in the occupied West Bank and Gaza Strip. For *Oz VeShalom* the cost of retaining these territories is too great if Israel desires to remain faithful to Jewish values. Unlike the *Gush Emunim* who believe that the Jewish people have a divine right to this land, *Oz*

VeShalom argues that no religious claims can justify such a policy. In a statement of its view, this movement declared:

> For us to live in peace and security in that cherished home-
> land, and to help Jewish culture to flourish by its contact with
> both the earth and the peoples of the Land, we Israelis must
> arrive at some kind of political compromise in which human
> sovereignty over God's Holy Land is shared with our Palestin-
> ian neighbours (as quoted in Ellis, 1987, 56–7).

Again, moral renewal is also manifest in the United States in acts of Jewish civil disobedience. In August 1985 Phyllis Taylor, a member of the Jewish Peace Fellowship, led a protest against nuclear weapons in the Nevada desert. Another Jewish activist Todd Kaplan and others entered the Martin Marietta factory in Orlando, Florida, poured blood on equipment and damaged sections of nuclear missiles with hammers. In an interview after this event, Kaplan stressed the Jewish roots of his involvement. 'I believe that the elimination of nuclear arms is a goal that we, as Jews, should embrace . . . We, as Jews, can't stand by passively and see the values that we hold dear go down the drain' (as quoted in Ellis, 1987, 60).

Another form of civil disobedience is the refusal to pay portions of income that go to the military. Rabbi Michael Robinson and his wife, for example, believe that such resistance fulfils the obligations of the Jewish tradition. 'We refuse to contribute to death and destruction. We give our energy, our efforts and our resources to the work of peace. We believe in the commandment, "Thou shalt not kill" ' (as quoted in Ellis, 1987, 61).

A final renewal in Jewish life is the feminist movement. Within Orthodox, Conservative and Reform Judaism, feminists are engaged in an active struggle to confront discrimi-
nation against women. In 1976 *Lilith* magazine was founded to foster this quest, and in subsequent years many Jewish feminist organizations have been established. These feminists organize shelters for battered women, hold con-
ferences, publish books and articles and press for child care and employment opportunities for women. In

addition, some feminists have attempted to use Jewish ritual to enhance the status of women, such as the *Brit B'not Yisrael* service which celebrates the entry of an infant girl to the covenant of Israel. The quest to incorporate feminism into the Jewish tradition is of critical importance to these activists. In the words of Paula Hyman, Dean of the College of Jewish Studies of the Jewish Theological Seminary:

> If the subordination of women is at the core of Judaism, then Judaism doesn't deserve to survive. As a feminist, I am not willing to accept my subordination and the subordination of my daughters and sisters as the price of Jewish tradition (as quoted in Ellis, 1987, 64).

According to Ellis, these movements of renewal in contemporary society constitute a major development within Judaism. Those who seek a redirection of Jewish life are attempting to be faithful to Jewish values. Though they are in the minority, they represent a central dimension of the Jewish faith. In the face of empowerment and nationhood, modern Judaism is being called to account. What emerged from the Holocaust was a shattered witness. What is needed today is prophetic testimony and commitment to the liberation of all who are oppressed and exploited by the Pharaohs of the modern age.

Liberation Theologies

Ellis notes that such religious revival in Judaism has strong parallels with the transformation taking place within the Christian community. The theme of the Exodus and the prophetic tradition within liberation theology have had a profound effect on Christian attitudes. Black liberation theology, for example, has used biblical concepts in propounding its message of freedom and justice. In *Black Theology and Black Power*, James Cone, the foremost black liberation theologian, notes that the ancient Israelites came to know God through the Exodus. It was God who emancipated the Jewish people from Egyptian bondage and subsequently established a covenant with his chosen people:

> Israel as a people initially came to know God through the Exodus. It was Yahweh who emancipated her from Egyptian bondage and subsequently established a covenant with her at Sinai . . . Divine righteousness means that God will be faithful to his promise, that his purposes for Israel will not be thwarted. Israel therefore need not worry about her weakness and powerlessness in a world of mighty military powers, 'for all the earth is mine' (Exodus 19:5). The righteousness of God means that he will protect her from the ungodly menacing of other nations. Righteousness means God is doing justice, that he is putting right what men have made wrong (Cone, 1972, 44).

According to Cone, divine righteousness means that God will be faithful to his promise. The Hebrew Scriptures provide a key to the understanding of his people's history and hopes for liberation. In the Bible God is involved in the struggle for deliverance – the account of the redemption of the ancient Israelites is also the story of the deliverance of an African people enslaved in America. For Cone, the Exodus is the key to understanding Jesus – through the Incarnation, God in Christ came to the weak and helpless.

In addition to Black liberation theology, liberation movements in South America have used central themes of the Jewish tradition in formulating their response to oppression. These writers emphasize that the Jewish people felt God's presence when he delivered them from oppression. At the Conference of Latin American Bishops at Medellin in Columbia in 1968, the Exodus was used as a framework for understanding God's action:

> Just as Israel of old, the first people [of God], felt the saving presence of God when he delivered them from the oppression of Egypt by passing through the sea and led them to the promised land, so we also, the new People of God, cannot cease to feel His saving presence in view of true development which is the passage for each and all from conditions of life

that are less human, to those that are more human (as quoted in Ellis, 1987, 70).

Several years later the Peruvian theologian Gustavo Gutiérrez published *A Theology of Liberation* in which he linked faith in God with just action. God, he argues, is a liberator who acts on behalf of struggling peoples. According to Gutiérrez, the liberation of Israel was the beginning of the construction of a just and fraternal society. God sent Moses to bring about the redemption of his chosen people: 'I have indeed seen the misery of My people in Egypt. I have heard their outcry against their slave masters. I have taken heed of their sufferings, and have come down to rescue them from the power of Egypt' (Exod. 3:7–9).

> The liberation of Israel is a political action. It is the breaking away from a situation of despoliation and misery and the beginning of the construction of a just and fraternal society. It is the suppression of disorder and the creation of a new order. The initial chapters of Exodus describe the oppression in which the Jewish people lived in Egypt, in that 'land of slavery' (13:3; 20:2; Deut. 5:6)' repression (1:10–11), alienated work (5:6–14), humiliations (1:13–14), enforced birth control policy (1:15–22). Yahweh then awakens the vocation of a liberator: Moses (Gutiérrez, 1973, 157).

For Gutiérrez it is within this biblical account as well as the evolution of prophecy that the true message of Jesus can be understood. For Gutiérrez, Jesus was a person who confronted the established political powers. His account of the Kingdom reveals the aspiration for a just society of peace and brotherhood.

The Hebrew Bible is also being used by Korean Christians who are developing their own theological position. Minjung Theology – a movement based on the experience of the masses – has developed from the experience of a people living under an unjust political régime. In the words of the Korean theologian Suh Kwang-Sun David:

> Theology of Minjung is a creation of those Christians who were forced to reflect upon their Christian discipleship in basement interrogation rooms, in trials, facing court martial

tribunals, hearing the allegation of prosecutors, and in making their own final defence. They reflected on their Christian commitment in prison cells, in their letters from prison to families and friends, in their readings of books sent by their friends all over the world, in their unemployment, in their stay at home under house arrest, while subject to a twenty-four-hour watch over their activities, and during visits with their friends (as quoted in Ellis, 1987, 72–3).

These individuals who reflect on Christian commitment in such terrible circumstances desire to share what they have learned with others who are similarly searching for a relevant theology in Asia. The theologian Moon Hee-Suk Cyris, for example, contends that the Minjung of today are confronting circumstances similar to those faced by the ancient Israelites. He writes:

Like Moses, Amos and Micah we in Korea must resolve to follow the footsteps of the true prophet living among our oppressed people and standing against political, social and economic oppression. To work for the transformation of our society is to participate in the task of ushering in the Kingdom of God (Ellis, 1987, 73).

The Jewish Response to Liberation Theology

Ellis points out that the reaction of the Jewish community to these liberation movements has been one of either ignorance, criticism or dismissal. What is needed is for Jews to go beyond these attitudes. It might appear that the theological task of dialogue between the post-Holocaust Jewish community and the theology of liberation is impossible – God did not rescue the Jewish people from the death camps, yet liberationists believe that He will lead them to freedom and justice. Nevertheless Ellis believes there are important parallels between the Holocaust experience and the struggle for liberation. It is possible, he writes, that by recounting the vision of the Holocaust victims we might be able to provide the basis for those who are today peering into the darkness with fear and trepidation (Ellis, 1987, 80).

Here Ellis cites the example of the death and abandonment of a Jewish mother of Eastern Europe, and then the same fate that befell a pastoral worker in Guatemala:

When I came up to the place we saw people naked lined up. But we were still hoping that this was only torture. Maybe there is hope – hope of living . . . One could not leave the line, but I wished to see – what are they doing on the hillock? Is there anyone down below? I turned my head and saw that some three or four rows were already killed on the ground. There were some twelve people amongst the dead. I also want to mention what my child said while we were lined up in the Ghetto, she said, 'Mother, why did you make me wear the Shabbat dress; we are going to be shot,' and when we stood near the dug-outs, near the grave, she said, 'Mother, why are we waiting, let us run!' Some of the young people tried to run, but they were caught immediately, and they were shot right there.

I had my daughter in my arms and ran after the truck. There were mothers who had two or three children and held them in their arms running after the truck. We ran all the way. There were those who fell – we were not allowed to help them rise. They were shot right there wherever they fell . . . When we all reached the destination, the people from the truck were already down and they were undressed – all lined up. All my family were there – undressed, lined up. The people from the truck, those who arrived before us . . . When it came to our turn, our father was beaten. We prayed, we begged with my father to undress, but he would not undress, he wanted to keep his underclothes. He did not want to stand naked. Then they tore off the clothing of the old man and he was shot. I saw it with my own eyes. And then they took my mother, and she said, let us go before her; but they caught mother and shot her too; and then there was my grandmother, my father's mother standing there; she was eighty years old and she had two children in her arms. And then there was my father's sister. She also had children in her arms and she was shot on the spot with the babies in her arms (as quoted in Ellis, 1987, 80–1).

All day long we were fleeing. We ran seeking the ravines. We brought all the injured from the other villages; there were many. The largest number were women and little children.

We hid in the mountains, but the women wore clothes of many colours, and from the helicopters they could see us very well. We saw the helicopters begin to fly in circles, surrounding us all. They began to machine-gun the people. The only way of saving ourselves was to run to the ravine and throw ourselves into it, which was quite steep. We began to run and run to the mountain, falling and falling. The small children ran alone. They were being left behind, getting lost among so many people, and all shouted, 'Mama, Mama'. One woman cried; she cried a lot, talking in the language of the Quiche. I didn't understand well what she said. Someone said to me, 'She's crying because her child was killed.' I had seen the little child. She had been born 15 days earlier. The woman had carried the child on her back. She fell when she was running, and she fell on the child and it was killed. She said, 'God is going to punish me. I have a great sin on me because I have killed my child.' A woman said, 'God is not with us, God has abandoned us. If we haven't done anything bad, if we haven't asked for so much, why does God abandon us now?' (as quoted in Ellis, 1987, 81–2).

The commonality in these experiences does not diminish the particular sufferings involved in the Holocaust and struggle for liberation. Yet what binds Jewish people and those who are currently exploited and oppressed is the universal characteristic of human misery. In religious terms the inability of many contemporary Jews to see a connection between their suffering and that of others is a form of idolatry – a perception that has atrophied in the Jewish community. It is not the idolatry of false gods, but the idolatry that is possible only from within the worship of the true God. Citing the words of the Chilean biblical scholar Pablo Richard, Ellis writes:

In Exodus 32 God reveals His transcendence as God the liberator, and not a God who consoles the oppressed so that they will accept their condition as an oppressed people. The veneration of God as consoler is idolatry. The seat or throne of this god . . . is gold, and gold is the symbol of domination (Ellis, 1987, 89).

Similarly, the biblical prophets criticized the people for

worshipping the false gods of domination and excessive materialism.

According to Ellis, parts of the Jewish community have their own idols today: capitalism, patriotism, and national security. What is required is for Jews to abandon such false gods. The refusal to engage in idolatry might actually begin healing the Jewish community; it could serve as a bridge between religious and secular Jews. Further, abandoning idolatrous practices can also link Jews with other communities which are enduring hardship. Jews and Christian liberationists can thus find common ground in their pursuit of God's Kingdom, and such openness to the hardships of others can draw the Jewish people back to their biblical origins. In this way liberation movements can serve as a source of religious renewal among Jews who are in search of authentic Jewish values.

Reconstructing Jewish Life

After the terrors of the Holocaust, the world has been emptied of values and goodness. As Hannah Arendt notes in *The Origins of Totalitarianism*, the Judeo-Christian tradition as well as humanism collapsed in the death camps. According to Arendt what is now required is a new philosophical and political structure that will renew Western culture. After nearly five decades, the need for such an enterprise still exists. Today, Ellis asserts, many see the possibility of a new foundation for Western civilization in the renewal of the traditions that collapsed during the Nazi onslaught. Christian liberationists are addressing this issue, and a new Christian witness has emerged in the latter half of the twentieth century – this new movement lends strength, courage and insight to struggling communities.

Similarly within the Jewish community, a number of Jews are struggling with the dialectics of Holocaust and empowerment. According to Ellis, what is now needed is Jewish solidarity with those who suffer:

The desire to be in solidarity does not eliminate the dynamics

of the Jewish community but places them in a different perspective. It has the possibility of moving us beyond isolation
and liberal concern into an active community that finds its
way by means of concrete acts of justice (Ellis, 1987, 93).

Such solidarity is both a journey outward and within – it
is an attempt to discover our own humanity in common
cause with those who are still enslaved.

Such solidarity also involves the willingness to enter into
history with authenticity. Jews who reach out to those at
the margin of society are engaging in a critical dialogue
with economic, social, political and religious issues. Such
a quest is a living witness which deepens the dialogue with
a reality which calls for commitment. In this struggle the
past is alive in the present through memory and myth,
shaping the lives and thoughts of the Jewish people. In
particular the Holocaust and the founding of the Jewish
State constitute the fundamental elements of this recon-
structed faith. Now that Jewry has become empowered in
its own land, the memory of the nation's enslaved ancestors
must be continually present. According to Ellis, 'those who
are empowered must bear in mind that solidarity with
those suffering in the present is the only link with suffering
in the past, and to ignore or cause suffering is to lose the
raison d'être of empowerment' (Ellis, 1987, 95).

To recover the memory of suffering, one must analyse
what has been elevated to the sacred. Two modern writers
whose views challenge present Jewish presuppositions were
Etty Hillesum and Martin Buber; in different ways, they
grappled with the formative events of contemporary Jewish
lives. Born in 1914, Hillesum was raised in the Netherlands
where she studied law and Slavonic languages. When she
began writing her diaries, the Netherlands were increasingly dominated by Nazi Germany. After the surrender
in 1940, Dutch Jews were gathered into ghettos and work-
camps; in 1942 they were forced to wear the Star of David
and began to be transported to transit camps. In the same
year, Hillesum became a typist in a department of the
Jewish Council. Two weeks after she began work, she

volunteered to go with the first group of Jews to Esterbork, a transit camp in the east of the country. There she remained until September 1943 when she was transported to Auschwitz, where she died. In her diaries, she explored the nature of suffering and compassion:

> They are merciless, totally without pity. And we must be all the more merciful ourselves. That's why I prayed early this morning: 'Oh God, times are too hard for frail people like myself. I know that a new and kinder day will come. I would so much like to live on, if only to express all the love I carry with me' (Hillesum, 1985, ix).

In another passage Hillesum stressed that human beings must join with God in safeguarding His divine presence:

> One thing is becoming increasingly clear to me: that You cannot help us, that we must help You to help ourselves. And that is all we can manage these days and also all that really matters: that we manage the safeguard that little piece of You, God in ourselves. And perhaps in others as well. Alas, there doesn't seem to be much You Yourself can do about our circumstances, about our lives. Neither do I hold You responsible. You cannot help us but we must help You and defend Your dwelling place inside us to the last (Hillesum, 1985, 186–7).

According to Ellis, such sentiments from a Holocaust victim are of profound significance. In her reflections, Hillesum asserts that fidelity with suffering opens the possibility for renewal and transformation. 'It is in the midst of suffering and commitment,' he writes, 'that Hillesum understands the beauty of creation and the goodness of life. The Kingdom of Death remains, though permeated with the sacredness of creation' (Ellis, 1987, 100–1). For Hillesum hatred was not a possibility – rather in suffering she was able to find hope and faith.

Another important voice from the recent Jewish past is that of the Jewish theologian Martin Buber. Rather than succumb to despair in the face of the Holocaust, Buber believed that Jewish renewal is possible through human reconciliation. Confronting the problem of Jewish empowerment in the land of Israel, Buber maintained that in returning to their homeland Jews were obligated to insure justice for all. 'Jewish settlement,' he stated, 'must not cause the political status of the present inhabitants to deteriorate; rather it must continue to ameliorate their economic condition.' Jewish settlers must therefore strive to live peacefully with their Arab neighbours and co-operate with them in developing the land. Throughout his life Buber struggled for such a policy of bi-nationalism.

In different ways both Hillesum and Buber advocated a path of hope and solidarity in a shattered world. After the Holocaust and the creation of a Jewish State such optimism may seem naïve, yet these writers caution us that hatred and isolation lead to a betrayal of the Jewish heritage. As Ellis explains:

> The *raison d'être* of empowerment found in the struggle and generosity of enslaved ancestors is in danger of being lost. The lives of Hillesum and Buber echo the challenge of Walter Benjamin to rescue tradition from conformity to power, a power that becomes the tool of the ruling class. They suggest that to move from one oppression to another, in spite of the rationale, is to forget our history and, ultimately to denigrate ourselves as a people (Ellis, 1987, 109).

Jewish Liberation Theology after the Holocaust

Today the Jewish community is struggling with the dialectics of Holocaust and empowerment, survival and ethics, and exile and renewal. According to Ellis, what is needed in contemporary society is Jewish solidarity with those who suffer. Through such commitment, Jews should be able to reclaim their own humanity. The journey towards others, he writes, is at the same time a journey towards the foundations of one's own community. In this light Ellis outlines a programme for contemporary Jewish theology:

> Holocaust theology is awaiting a new theology . . . today a new generation of Jewish theologians is needed. Buoyed up by the movements of ethical concern and renewal . . . they

67

must emerge from the periphery of Jewish life to challenge a consensus that admits little dissent (Ellis, 1987, 111).

This new Jewish theology, he believes, should have a number of characteristics. First, it must respond to a self-critical voice that comes from the depths of the Jewish tradition and seeks to serve others. It should be distinctly Jewish, yet generous towards other religious and humanist communities. Moreover, it needs to acknowledge that genuine affirmation comes only through critical discourse and responsible activity. It must be present in history rather than pretending to isolation or transcendence. Further, Jewish theology must be inclusive in the search for a renewal of communal life in the midst of the Holocaust and empowerment. It must refuse to be silent despite pressure from political and religious neo-conservatives. Jewish theology must also balance the survival of the Jewish people with the preservation of its message of community. Again, Jewish theology requires the recovery of Jewish witness against modern idolatry. Finally, Jewish theology must be a call to repentance and solidarity with those who suffer.

Such a Jewish theology of liberation is based on the revival of the prophetic dimensions of the Jewish faith. The prophetic and liberation themes of the Jewish heritage confront the dialectic of Holocaust and empowerment and emphasize aspects of Judaism which have been overshadowed in the modern world. This theology of liberation can act as a catalyst to break through the paralysis confronting the Jewish community. According to Ellis, the people of Guatemala, Nicaragua, El Salvador, and those struggling for freedom in South America can join in this rediscovery. He asks:

> Could it be that in our struggle we are not alone, but are living rather in a broader tradition of faith and struggle, one that now seeks to galvanize the witness of each community or to share it with other struggling communities in a common struggle for liberation? (Ellis, 1987, 113).

A Jewish theology of liberation must insist that the issue

of anti-Semitism be confronted; yet at the same time it should not use anti-Semitism as an ideological weapon. The slogan 'Never Again' is often used as a rationale for avoiding moral responsibility. Jews should not be blinded to the fact that Palestinians and Arabs are being discriminated against by Israelis. The same is true with respect to American Blacks. Although anti-Semitism exists in the Black community, Jews should not ignore the racism that keeps Blacks at the margins of society. Jews are not absolved of responsibility even if they are victims of prejudice. Anti-Semitism should not be a shield that deflects important questions for the Jewish community today. Rather, a Jewish theology of liberation needs to turn the facts of anti-Semitism into a challenge for critical reflection.

Concerning the problem of empowerment, a Jewish theology of liberation should insist that others should have the same rights as Jews. Palestinians deserve a State and Israel ought to participate in its establishment. 'The Palestinian people', Ellis writes, 'have been deeply wronged in the creation of Israel and in the occupied territories. As we celebrate our empowerment, we must repent our transgressions' (Ellis, 1987, 116). Similarly, a Jewish theology of liberation must also question Jewish empowerment in the USA. The Jewish community looks to the USA to guarantee Israel's security, but the cost of such a guarantee is not discussed. Jewish ethics should empel Jews to seek solidarity with others; *Realpolitik*, however, sees the interests of the poor in the First and Third World as threats to a system that works to the advantage of the Jewish people.

According to Ellis, impoverished Jews are a part of the past that the Jewish community wants to bury, since they represent the ghetto experience. Leading neo-conservative Norman Podhoretz, for example, woke up one morning and realized it is better to be rich and powerful than poor and weak. Such a view, however, overlooks how wealth is created. Power demands the weakness of others – oligarchy is the reality of modern life. Capitalism provides affluence for the few, but it involves unemployment and poverty for the majority. A Jewish theology of liberation involves a critique of the economic structure of contemporary society. A Jewish theology of liberation should also be of significance for secular activists who have abandoned traditional Jewish life. Their criticism of political and economic power embodies Jewish ethics without a religious language. Paradoxically many of those Jews on the left who were uninterested in the Jewish faith embraced traditional ideals, while those who prayed worshipped the idols of contemporary life.

Today this division can be overcome. Religious Jews can be nourished by the Jewish tradition. As Ellis asks, 'What is a religious Jew if not one who transforms the world because of his or her faith? And what is a secular Jewish leftist if not a practising Jew without a portfolio?' In this regard, a Jewish theology of liberation can make a contribution to Holocaust theology. Holocaust theologians have redefined the concept of a practising Jew from one who observes the law to one who cherishes memory and survival. A Jewish theology of liberation adds to that definition the pursuit of justice and peace.

A Jewish theology of liberation must also insist that indentification with Israel is not in itself a religious act. The State of Israel is a flawed attempt to create a presence in the Middle East. A Jewish liberationist would therefore deny that Jewish history revolves around a return to the land. It is thus a mistake to identify Zionism with Judaism. Zionists are those who have settled in Israel. Those living in the diaspora who believe that Israel is the centre of their Jewish identity are Israelites or Israeli-identified Jews. Though the majority of the Jewish people may be Israeli-identified, they are not Zionists. Thus Zionism and Judaism are not synonymous terms. Indeed, Ellis stresses that the Jewish people existed before the State of Israel and will continue long after the nation ceases to exist. In this connection Ellis maintains that when Jews enter into dialogue with Christians, they should not demand uncritical support for Israel. Instead they should explore together the possibilities for solidarity with those who suffer.

According to Ellis, by witnessing to their history Jews can contribute to contemporary struggles for liberation. Jews, he believes, are called to this task:

> The celebration of our Exodus from Egypt, the Passover, again contains lessons: we mourn the loss of Egyptian blood shed for our liberation and are cautioned on our most festive holiday to recall the strangers in our own midst for we were strangers in a strange land (Ellis, 1987, 121–2).

A Jewish theology of liberation offers a vision for all people 5,000 years of history provide a foundation upon which to build a future. In the post-Holocaust period, the world needs this witness, and at the crossroads of their history, he writes, so do the Jewish people.

3 Jewish and Christian Responses

The arguments which Marc Ellis and I put forward advocating the formulation of a Jewish theology of liberation have stimulated a variety of responses. While some Jews and Christians supported this project, others raised serious doubts about its feasibility. According to these Jewish critics, Christian liberation theologians have perpetrated stereotypical anti-Semitic attitudes in their writings. In 1991 Orbis Books published a collection of such criticisms (as well as responses by defenders of Jewish liberation theology) in a volume entitled: *Judaism, Christianity and Liberation: An Agenda for Dialogue* edited by Otto Maduro (who teaches at the Maryknoll School of Theology). This volume is intended to advance the dialogue between Christians and Jews and provide a basis for further reflection about the nature of liberation theology on the threshold of the twenty-first century. Its various contributions illuminate the evolution of this new theological development within the Jewish world over the last few years.

Jewish Responses to Liberation Theology

In his essay 'Liberation Theology and Judaism' published in *Judaism, Christianity and Liberation*, Judd Kruger Levingston, of the Jewish Theological Seminary, points out that many Jewish thinkers are reluctant to embrace liberation theology because of the misunderstandings of Jews, Judaism and Israel that are found in the works of liberationists. Such distortion, Levingston believes, is due to the fact that Christian liberation theologians live in areas where there are few Jews. Further, when these writers were students in Europe in the 1950s and 1960s, their theological studies were infused with the Christian doctrine of successionism and such ideas passed into their own writings. Thus, anti-Judaism has inadvertently become an inherent feature of this new theological movement.

Hence in *A Theology of Liberation* Gustavo Gutiérrez depicts Judaism as corrupt:

> When the infidelities of the Jewish people rendered the Old Covenant invalid, the Promise was incarnated both in the proclamation of a New Covenant, which was awaited and sustained by the 'remnant', as well as in the promises which prepared and accompanied its advent (Gutiérrez, 1973, 161).

Again, Naim Ateek, a Palestinian Christian theologian, emphasizes the Jewish people's rejection of Jesus, echoing the sentiments of the Fourth Gospel:

> [Jesus] came to his own home and his own people received him not. But to all who received him, who believed in his name, he gave power to become children of God; who were born, not of blood nor of the will of the flesh nor of the will of man, but of God (Ateek, 1989, 172).

In this context the Costa Rican theologian Victorio Araya continues the negative depiction of the Pharisees found in the New Testament:

> Jesus proclaims God's transcendence in his discussions with the Pharisees – for example in accusing them of seeking to manipulate God through human traditions (Mark 7:1–17). His defence of that transcendence is all the more remarkable in that these traditions through which Jesus' interlocutors 'nullify God's word', are religious traditions (Mark 7:13) (Araya, 1987, 69).

A number of Jewish and Christian thinkers have stressed that liberationists need to purge themselves of such sentiments. Leon Klenicki, Director of the Department of Interfaith Affairs of the Anti-Defamation League of Bnai B'rith, for example, insists that liberation theology lacks a true understanding of Judaism. By ignoring the significance of the *mitzvot* (divine commandments) liberationists do not perceive the link between the Jewish people and God. Further, he accuses liberation theologians of abandoning the Jewish people after the time of the Exodus: 'Liberation thinkers freeze Judaism at the time of leaving Egypt. It would seem that Jews are only Jews when enslaved' (Klenicki, 1988, 8). According to Klenicki, it is a tragedy to disregard two thousand years of religious development.

Jews have also been critical of the liberationists' belief that God exercises a preferential option for the poor. Thus Jon Levinson of the Harvard Divinity School writes that although the Torah sides with those who are exploited, 'oppression, poverty, and suffering were not thought to qualify one for inclusion in the chosen people' (as quoted by Judd Kruger Levingston, 1991, 9). God freed the Jewish people not because they were enslaved, but for the sake of the covenant. According to Levingston, the liberationists' emphasis on God's concern for the poor leads to a new form of supersessionism: 'The story of the Exodus has been rewritten under the pressure of the crises of the poor in the Third World; now the Jews have been left out of their own foundational story, superseded by the poor and the oppressed, as they were once superseded by the communion of the baptized' (as quoted by Levingston, 1991, 10).

Another objection to liberation theology relates to the fact that Jews rarely engage in the type of systematic universalistic theology espoused by liberationists. According to Levingston, the Jewish relationship with God is expressed primarily through inner faith and personal commitments:

> Jews examine ethical issues, interpersonal relations, and religious behaviour in the *Talmud* and codes. God's relationship with the Jews continues to be played out in daily behaviour and in the continuing evolution of humanity. In contrast, for the liberation theologians, God's will seems to be made clearest in the success of a cataclysmic event such as a revolution.' (Levingston, 1991, 12).

Hence the approach of liberation theologians to society's problems is foreign to Jewish categories of thought.

A final criticism of liberation theology concerns the liberationists' endorsement of socialism. Given such political leanings, a number of Jews fear that movements of national liberation or national socialism will lead to the type of totalitarian regimes and anti-Semitic uprisings that took place in Nazi Germany, Stalinist Russia, and recently Eastern Europe. Such socialist attitudes have also led to criticism of the State of Israel, particularly in relation to the plight of the Palestinians. For many critics, such a negative depiction of the Jewish homeland is a fundamental defect of liberation theology: by pleading for the liberation of the poor in the Middle East, further Jewish suffering has been encouraged by the left.

The Judeo-Christian Tradition and Human Liberation

In the chapter 'Liberation Theology: A Political Expression of Biblical Faith' in *Judaism, Christianity and Liberation* (ed. Maduro, 1991) the South American theologian Leonardo Boff argues that both Judaism and Christianity have a role in the creation of a better future in the Americas. This task, he believes, has become increasingly urgent in the aftermath of the Holocaust. For Boff, humanity must engage in a struggle to ensure that the human oppression of innocent victims – including the annihilation of Jews in Nazi extermination camps – never occurs again. Such a quest presupposes that historical evil must be transcended by a practical alternative which makes further repetitions impossible.

In support of this initiative Boff turns to those aspects of the biblical narrative which are open to the themes of liberation. According to Boff, everything occurs beneath God's gaze – nothing lies outside His providential plan. Thus he writes:

As a God who is alive, this God is extremely sensitive to all those who feel themselves threatened in their lives and cry out for life. Because of this the Bible bears witness always that God is one who hears the cry of the oppressed and takes part in the struggle for liberation (Ex. 3:4–7). God is the God of the Outcry. The faithful know that if they cry out for life, justice and liberty, God will be listening to them and supporting all that may be done to create more liberty, justice and life (Boff, 1991, 27).

Because God is sensitive to the cry of the afflicted, He abhors iniquity and seeks justice. The promise of a future life and the redemption of all people is an eternal hope which unites the entire created order.

In espousing this view, Boff appeals to the Exodus as a paradigm for God's liberating action. Quoting the Medellin document which inaugurated the theology of liberation in the 1960s, Boff writes:

As in ancient times Israel, the first people, experienced the presence of God who saves, when he freed them from the oppression of Egypt, so also we, the new people of God, cannot fail to hear his step which saves when true development takes place. It is a case then for each one and for all, of passing from less human conditions of life to those which are more human (Boff, 1991, 28).

In this narrative, faith and politics are untied. In the Exodus the two principal moments of any liberation process are apparent: liberation-from (the oppression of Pharaoh), and liberation-to (entry into the Promised Land). When the people of Israel escaped from bondage, they gained their identity, and this primal event in the history of the nation became the fulcrum of the people's faith. It composed the nucleus of the Jewish creed, which was always recited when the first-fruits of the land were presented (Deut. 26:5–9). Similarly, in the New Testament the Good News of Jesus can be understood only if the devout know the God whom he calls Father: 'For him as for the other Jews, this God is "he who brought us out of Egypt, from the house of slavery" ' (Boff, 1991, 28).

Thus the Exodus provides a framework for understanding God's action in the world. Since the Christian community regards itself as a continuation of the biblical people, they are assured that God will also hear their cries of affliction. For the Christian, liberation does not consist in establishing a homeland in the Promised Land but rather in transcending death and transfiguring the entire universe. As Boff writes, the Exodus is 'the journey of the whole of humanity and of creation toward the resurrection of all flesh and the renewal of heaven and earth' (Boff, 1991, 28). In practical terms such a process is manifest in a preferential option for the poor. This shift in gravity away from institutionalized religion calls for a total re-evaluation of Christian values. No longer should the Church attempt to reinforce the status quo – it must direct its attention to those at the margin of society.

Such a preferential option involves trying to understand social reality and history from the standpoint of those at the bottom. From the perspective of those who are impoverished, society must be transformed so as to bring about justice and equality. In choosing this option the churches need to alter their priorities and adopt a critical stance toward the ruling system. From this vantage point, the church must be rebellious and subversive. Further, the option for the poor implies the assumption of the cause of those who are deprived of life's fullness:

> This cause is linked to the fundamental satisfaction of the basic necessities of life: work, shelter, clothing, health, education, and so forth. The poor do not dream of a country which is a great power, dominating others; neither do they wish for Pharaoh-like riches and consumerism. They want those conditions which will allow them a decent life, based on work and political participation (Boff, 1991, 30).

Boff also contends that the option for the poor involves the perception that the subjects of liberation are the oppressed themselves. Neither the State nor the Churches are capable of resolving the problems of the poor – rather the disadvantaged must embark on this task. The struggle of transformation as well as the type of society that is to result must be determined by those who suffer exploitation and oppression. None the less it is possible, Boff believes, to envisage the mode of society which is required to liberate the masses. Some theologians have espoused socialism as the system under which the ideals of liberation can flourish. Yet Boff contends that socialism in practice has frequently produced an immense paternalistic State which does a great deal for the people, but does not advance their critical participation. Thus Boff advocates participatory democracy as the ideal model for society. Such a social order, he believes, should be based on four fundamental principles: (1) the most open participation possible; (2) equality which results from the participation of all; (3) respect for diversity; and (4) the communion which results from the search for united human relationships.

In conclusion Boff emphasizes that the theology of liberation is rooted in the biblical tradition. Inspired by the message of the Hebrew Scriptures, many Christians today are dedicated to building a new society in which all people will be able to live together with dignity. Biblical faith, however, is not limited to this social function; it also promises eternal life. Such a promise is anticipated by God's plan for humanity – hence the biblical tradition can unite Jews and Christians in a common quest to bring about the realization of God's plan for redemption. 'The existence of liberation theology', he writes, 'proves that it is possible to keep alive the liberating memory of the Bible and of God's promise to always listen to the cry of the oppressed' (Boff, 1991, 32).

Jews, Christians and Liberation Theology

The recovery of the biblical roots of Christian liberation theology is the central theme of the Chilean theologian Pablo Richard's contribution, 'Jewish and Christian Liberation Theology', in *Judaism, Christianity and Liberation*. He notes that biblical Israel gave birth to Christianity. Thus rabbinic Judaism and Christianity are inextricably interrelated. Yet despite such a common heritage, these two religious systems have been antagonists throughout their history. In the modern era Western Christendom has been responsible for the Jewish Holocaust, whereas the State of Israel is guilty of persecuting the Palestinian population. In their different ways both faiths have been unfaithful to their origins. He writes:

> Christianity betrayed itself by becoming the religion of the empire, first of the Roman Empire, and then of all the empires that dominated the West. Judaism also finally betrayed itself by becoming the oppressor state and the ally of the worst imperialism of all times, North American imperialism (Richard, 1991, 33).

What is now required is for both religions to return to their true identity, rediscover their biblical roots, and cease to victimize the innocent. From the Christian side, the Church should identify with those who have been oppressed by Western Christendom; Jews should similarly act in solidarity with the victims of Jewish aggression in Israel. Such solidarity is a primary principle of both faiths. In the Hebrew Scriptures the term *hesed* denotes the essence of divine and human action; it is translated as 'mercy', 'compassion', and 'pity'. The corresponding Greek term *agape* is best translated by 'solidarity' rather than 'love'. These two terms, taken together, express the ethics of the entire Judeo-Christian tradition. Hence the message of solidarity is a fundamental requirement of the religious life – one which can bind Jews and Christians together in a common cause.

In propounding this view, Richard points out that one of the most ancient heresies of the Christian past was that promulgated by Marcion which attempted to separate the Old from the New Testament. In contemporary society this heresy continues to permeate Christian theology: many Christians fail to recognize the significance of the Hebrew Bible, thereby denying the biblical roots of their own tradition. Such an attitude leads to a distortion of the Christian message, since the Old and New Testaments are dialectically related. As St Augustine explained, 'The New Testament is latent in the Old, and the Old patent in the

New.' What is of vital significance today are the prophetic dimensions of the Old Testament faith. For liberationists it is just this aspect of Scripture which must be recovered.

According to Richard, Christian anti-Semitism is due to the Church's separation from its Jewish roots. The hatred of Judaism and the Jewish people, he argues, is essentially a Christian creation even though it is manifest in secular terms in modern society. Judeophobia has been one of the most destructive forces of Western civilization. As an ideology it opposes the attainment of human freedom, and in this respect it runs counter to all forms of liberation. 'In sum,' Richard writes, 'anti-Semitism is identical with anti-messianism, and anti-utopianism, anti-communism, anti-popular liberation' (Richard, 1991, 36).

Given such an orientation, it is difficult to understand how Christianity (which emerged from the Jewish teaching about the Exodus and the prophetic tradition) could have betrayed its own heritage. Rather than break with tradition, Jesus sought to radicalize the prophetic, messianic and apocalyptic traditions of the faith. The conflict between Christianity and Judaism is thus based on a particular interpretation of Judaism. There is no inherent conflict between these two religions, rather the contradiction is between the Christian faith and Sadducean-Pharisaism.

Subsequent rivalry was not with Jews but with those Judaizers who believed in Jesus but nevertheless identified the Christian faith with the fulfilment of the Law. After the destruction of the Temple in AD 70, the rabbis expelled Christians from the synagogue due to their heretical views. Hence the conflict between these two faiths was generated by conflicting interpretations of the biblical tradition. Richard asserts:

> Christianity was not born from the rejection of the biblical-Jewish tradition – the exilic, messianic, prophetic, and apocalyptic traditions. On the contrary, it tried to radicalize those traditions. The critique that Jesus and later Paul made of the law and the temple is a critique that they made as good Jews, faithful to the biblical-Jewish tradition that goes back to the

faith of Abraham. In no way is their critique an anti-Semitic position (Richard, 1991, 37).

Christian anti-Judaism therefore emerged within Christendom despite the common ground between both faiths. Over the centuries the deicide charge and the Christian accusations that Jews have delayed the second coming by refusing to accept Christ have inflamed Christian hostility. Paradoxically this shift in perspective constitutes a rejection of true Christianity. What is now required is for Christians to recover the origins of Christianity that existed before the evolution of Western Christendom. Such a task of reconstruction should be accompanied by an exegesis in which ambiguous texts are recovered in their original meaning. Such an endeavour has already been undertaken by sociological study of the Bible particularly in the USA and by a popular liberationist interpretation reading in Latin America. This quest, Richard contends, should result in the re-creation of Christianity, understood as a Semitic religion infused with messianism, and prophetic and apocalyptic elements. For Richard this rereading of Christian origins can be enhanced by the formulation of a Jewish liberation theology. Christian and Jewish liberation theology, he maintains, can unite in solidarity with the poor and the oppressed. It is now a question of reconstituting the original Christian teaching into a liberated and liberating Christianity and of reshaping the biblical heritage of Judaism into a similar liberating message.

Holocaust and Liberation

Another Latin American contributor to *Judaism, Christianity and Liberation*, Julio de Santa Ana, focuses on the tension between oppression and liberation. The Jewish people, he notes, struggled for their own land across the centuries and eventually attained this goal after millions of victims had been murdered in the death camps. According to de Santa Ana, the creation of a Jewish State was stimulated by a general awareness of the right of oppressed peoples to their own self-determination. Unfortunately, however, it is often the case that the liberators of yesterday become the oppressors of today – a phenomenon clearly manifest in the State of Israel. Today, Jews who were previously subjugated and persecuted have become the oppressors of the Palestinian people.

This transition from powerlessness to empowerment has led to the abandonment of traditional Jewish values. In the Hebrew Scriptures, social concern is of paramount importance. Thus the Torah asserts that poverty is an evil rooted in oppressive, dependent relationships. For this reason Exodus stipulates that one must help the poor, the widow, the orphan, the foreigner and the slave (Exod. 21:1–11; 22:20–23). Such precepts characterize the social life of the nation as a federation of tribes concerned with the welfare of all. Injustice and oppression occur when individuals are allowed to take advantage of those who are marginalized in society. Such an orientation was reinforced by the prophets who defended the poor in fidelity to the covenant. Amos, for example, denounced suffocating taxes and interest (Amos 4:1; 5:11–12), fraudulent commerce (8:4–5), and numerous other abuses. Similarly Micah denounced the hoarding of lands (Mic. 2:1–3), and Isaiah condemned the corruption of authorities who issued decrees which favoured the powerful and crushed the weak (Isa. 10:1–2; 32:7).

According to the biblical tradition poverty is not simply a misfortune, but rather the fruit of injustice and oppression. The Torah prescribes that there should be no poor in Israel if God's commands are followed (Deut. 15:4). To do justice consists in helping the poor so that they can overcome the condition of poverty. In this respect, the Bible expresses a bias towards the poor. De Santa Ana insists that this attitude is expressed in numerous psalms: The poor are integral, right and just when they observe God's commandments (Ps. 34:16, 20, 22; 36:17–18):

Because of this, the 'poor of Yahweh' are God's friends. God's enemy is the proud person who tries to oppress the

poor and the weak, to take advantage of them. By doing so
the proud person ignores the presence and the challenge of
the other (de Santa Ana, 1991, 44).

This message, de Santa Ana believes, has been lost in
the contemporary Jewish response to the events of the
Holocaust. Understandably the Jewish community is dis-
mayed about the horrors of the Nazi régime. Unfortunately
the suffering of the Jewish people has intensified their
bitterness, and in their anger the nation had adopted
oppressive and unjust policies toward the Palestinian
people. Once an oppressed people, the Jews have become
the oppressors. As de Santa Ana explains:

> The oppressed, then, takes over the same orientation in life
> as the oppressor. If the oppressor sought to dominate the
> other, using any means possible, the oppressed almost mech-
> anically and unconsciously repeats the attitude of the domi-
> nator (de Santa Ana, 1991, 44–5).

What is now required is for the Jewish people to adopt a
theology of solidarity which is rooted in their ancient tradition. The emphasis of the faith should be on universal
concern rather than exclusivity. In the context of the
Middle East, the Palestinian people call for recognition
and dialogue. Solidarity with the Palestinians will demon-
strate that the Jewish people have been able to overcome
the tragedy of their recent past.

Drawing on the theme of the Exodus, de Santa Ana
stresses that the theology of liberation challenges contemporary Jewish theology. The State of Israel came into being
after the Nazi onslaught on the Jewish people. At that
time this new nation was weak and vulnerable, fearful that
the Holocaust could be repeated. Such factors led Israel
to adopt the behaviour of its former oppressors. Such a
policy was based on *Realpolitik*. Yet in its quest for internal
security, the State of Israel oppressed the Palestinian
masses and engaged in open war with the Arabs. Most
Jewish Holocaust theologians defend such reactionary attitudes. Here liberation theology must raise vital questions
for Jewry: How is it possible to keep alive the spirit of the

Exodus? How can the nation remain faithful to a vocation of freedom and justice?

According to de Santa Ana, this is not the first time that the Jewish people have set aside the spirit of the Exodus. In ancient Israel when the monarchy adopted policies of repression, the ideals of liberation and justice were forgotten. Similarly today he writes:

> We have the impression that an important sector is repeating the same experience, while the other sectors struggle to keep alive fidelity to the vocation of Israel. Those who opt to legitimate aggressiveness and authoritarian attitudes in some way express a spirit that represents the priesthood, producer of symbolic goods that nourished the nationalist and exclusivist aspirations of postexilic Judaism. They demand, as representatives of the priestly spirit, that there be sacrifice. Obviously the offering does not include the Jews. Today, unfortunately, the Palestinians are sacrificed (de Santa Ana, 1991, 50).

Such an attitude has proved profoundly troubling for many Christians, who are aware of the tragedy that befell the Jewish people during Nazi rule. When these Christians observe the Jewish people adopt dogmatic authoritarianism in Israel, they are uncertain whether they should continue to support a Jewish State. Conscious of the inheritance of the Exodus, they feel compelled to uphold the rights of the Palestinians to self-determination and freedom. Similarly in Israel there are Jews who are sympathetic to the plight of the Palestinian people. In this light de Santa Ana contends that the Jewish community must strive to ensure that Israeli institutions foster social development in consonance with the Torah. This is perhaps the greatest challenge facing world Jewry today. As he explains:

> It undoubtedly implies the demand to transcend the theology of the Holocaust, or a theology that is fundamentally priestly. It is a request that theology also free itself, that it cease to be exclusive, and that it live in a practical way the extension of the gift – a life that not only nourishes itself from memory,

but also, and especially, nourishes itself from promise. The promise of God that opens the future to all human beings (de Santa Ana, 1991, 51).

A Jewish Liberation Theology

In another essay in *Judaism, Christianity and Liberation*, the Jewish writer Michael Lerner adds a further contribution to the formulation of a Jewish theology of liberation. According to Lerner, it was not the rebellion of the ancient Israelites and their exodus from Egypt which made Judaism the historical source of revolutionary thought. Rather the narration of this pivotal event in the Torah and in every Sabbath celebration kept the Jewish people at the forefront of revolutionary innovation and social change. From ancient times to the present the nation insisted that human beings have the right to liberate themselves from the fetters of oppression. He writes:

> The notion that we are free to break the chains of the past, and that it is our obligation to do so, is the essence of the revolutionary message of Judaism. The domination of the past over the present is not inevitable, and through our own activity we can make things different – this is the spirit of the Torah that has permeated Jewish consciousness (Lerner, 1991, 57).

This message of liberation is linked with the Torah's insistence that those who have been oppressed do not become oppressors themselves. Thus Scripture decrees that when the Israelites conquer the land they do not re-create a world of oppression. No injunction is repeated more frequently in the Torah than the obligation not to oppress the stranger. Jews are to remember their own slavery and struggle to free those who are enslaved by the Pharaohs of later ages. Yet despite this duty, the Jewish people today have tragically been unable to transcend their recent past: in Israel the Palestinian people are trampled underfoot and denied their rights. Lerner notes that in contemporary society there are a significant number of Jews who are critical of such repressive policies. What these critics demand is for the nation to live up to the ideals of freedom which are inherent in the tradition.

In expounding this theses Lerner focuses on the biblical conception of a God who intervenes in history. Here he interprets God's name as revealed to Moses in the Book of Exodus – 'I shall be what I shall be' (Exod. 3:14) – as denoting the God whose very nature is the possibility of transcendence, freedom and self-determination. What is implied in this verse is that the past can be overcome; there is possibility in the universe for change in accord with our ability to hear the cry of the oppressed. God, he writes, does not passively submit to the pain and shed tears in heaven while remaining absent on earth. 'Rather, this is a God who has intervened in human history, through the agency of the Jewish people to give the message to the world that this pain and suffering can and ought to be ended' (Lerner, 1991, 59). The Jewish people, however, have not always been capable of responding to this divine decree. As Scripture records, the moment God revealed himself to Moses on Mount Sinai, the Israelites were building the golden calf. Instead of relying on the God of freedom, they wanted a god who could be seen and touched. Yet despite such failures, God calls His people to witness to the duty of justice and love – this divine obligation is as pressing today as it was in times past.

In attempting to fulfil this duty, it is imperative to differentiate between the voice of God and the self-deceptions of the age. In this context Lerner argues that over the past few centuries capitalist society has asserted that all persons are radically different and should therefore be valued as independent, self-determining individuals. Further, it is assumed that in entering human relationships, our highest obligation is to look after our own personal interests. Hence we are free to shape our lives as we wish – we have no one to blame except ourselves if we do not achieve personal satisfaction and fulfilment. These allegedly self-evident truths are embodied in the structure of the capitalist world. Yet, according to Lerner, such a conception of human potentiality is inherently flawed. It is preferable, he argues, to value our fellow human beings not simply for their unique characteristics, but for what all human beings have in common. In opposition to the capitalist understanding of human society, Lerner posits a world in which we are not set apart from each other but are necessarily linked so that our personal survival is inextricably bound up with the future of the human race. In such an environment loving concern rather than personal achievement would be the dominating motif.

The quest to discover such values, Lerner believes, is consonant with the tradition of Israel struggling with God to discern the divine voice.

> We are the embodiment of the collective experience of the human race, refracted through the specific experience of our nation, our people, and our own family, and shaped by the ideologies and forms of life that are available to us as we grow to maturity in a specific class society. Just as every generation before us has had its limitations when it approaches the divine, so do we. Just as every other generation has been overwhelmed by the spirit of the divine, run away from it, asked others to interpret it for us, so have we. We need only look at the way we abandoned the spirit of the 1960s to know how frightening it is to come face to face with the possibility that the world could be radically remade (Lerner, 1991, 63).

Such a struggle to discern the divine will is imperative in a world where the false gods of personal ambition, achievement and self-centredness dominate daily life. The message of the Torah is that human beings are partners with God in creating a better world: we are commanded to act in accord with the divine plan for a world based on love, justice and compassion. Today we must overcome self-doubt and scepticism in pursuit of this vision. The chains of history can be broken if we hearken to God's voice which echoes down the ages, challenging us to re-create the world so that exploitation and oppression cease to exist.

Jewish-Christian Solidarity

In her contribution to *Judaism, Christianity and Liberation*, the Christian theologian Rosemary Radford Ruether formulates a liberation theology of Jewish-Christian solidarity. In the Hebrew Scriptures, Ruether notes, the Jewish faith was both particularistic and universalistic in orientation. On the one hand, Israel was to separate itself from other peoples – the covenant bound the Jewish people to the worship of one God and the legal code separated Israel from the abominations of other nations. On the other hand, the tradition asserts that all peoples will come to redemption through Israel. In the words of Isaiah:

> It shall come to pass in the latter days that the mountain of the Lord shall be established as the highest of all the mountains . . . and all nations shall flow to it and many people shall come and say, 'Come let us go up to the Mountain of the Lord, to the house of the God of Jacob, that he may teach us his ways and that we may walk in his paths, for out of Zion shall go forth the law and the word of the Lord from Jerusalem' (Isa. 2:2–3).

The rabbinic tradition carried on this legacy by asserting that Jews were called to be a holy people obedient to God's laws while at the same time maintaining that the Jewish people are to be a harbinger of universal redemption and salvation.

In contrast with Judaism, Christianity has been a proselytizing religion. In the New Testament and the writings of the Church Fathers, the Jewish faith was viewed as anticipatory. As time passed Christians came to see themselves as the new universal people of God, and in their triumphalism they regarded the Jewish nation as a pariah people. Accused of deicide, Jews were marked like Cain, and destined to wander as exiles for all time. During the Reformation however, the Church began to reinterpret the relationship between Christians and Jews. Competing nation-states, with their nationalized churches, came to define themselves as the new Israel, whereas contemporary Jews were seen as representing the continuing election of the old Israel. In this light Protestants argued that the new Israel should sponsor the restoration of the old Israel to its former homeland; there they would regain their national sovereignty and rebuild the Temple. Once these particularistic aspirations were fulfilled, there would be a universal judgement and redemption through Christ. Not surprisingly within the Jewish world such messianic intentions were firmly rejected. Instead, in the nineteenth century there emerged a secular Jewish movement to return to Palestine which was motivated by the recognition that the Jews are fundamentally unassimiable into European society.

Despite the secularism and atheistic attitudes of most Zionist leaders, the Jewish community has come to endorse Zionist aspirations on religious grounds. Such a shift in orientation is largely due to the religious conviction that God promised to return the Jews to their homeland: on this basis world Jewry has supported the creation and continuation of a Jewish state. Such religious Zionism was endorsed by Rabbi Abraham Kook, the Ashkenazi chief rabbi of Palestine under the British mandate. Drawing on kabbalistic ideas, Kook saw the universe as fragmented by the cosmic fall into evil. These sparks, Kook believed, were the souls of Jews living in the diaspora – what is required is to draw these scattered sparks back to the holy land, in this way the souls of all Jews would be gathered to their divine centre. In such a Jewish state the Torah would become the law of the land and Israel would become a holy nation, capable of healing other peoples. The cosmic vision has been transformed into a more militant and ethnocentric conception by Kook's son, Rabbi Zvi Yehudah Kook and the *Gush Emunim*. These traditionalists have been at the forefront of the Jewish settlement of the occupied territories. In addition they have sponsored militant *yeshiva* students who aim to expand the Jewish section of the Old City of Jerusalem with the ultimate aim of taking over the Temple mount itself from Muslim guardians.

According to Reuther, such messianic Zionist theology is a false doctrine. Both Jews and Christians who have espoused this ideology on the basis of Jewish-Christian dialogue are becoming increasingly hostile and defensive. Rather than face the failings of such a view, they project their hatred of the outside world. Any Jew who seeks to criticize such Israeli politics is regarded as a self-hating Jew, and all gentile critics are branded anti-Semitics. Yet, there can be no authentic Jewish-Christian dialogue on this basis:

> A dialogue based on this theology has painted itself into a corner of pandering and mutual manipulation. Jewish-Christian dialogue, if it is to be authentic, must be refounded on a new basis. This basis I call a liberation theology of Jewish-Christian solidarity (Reuther, 1991, 90).

For Reuther such a new theology should be based on the recognition that both Jews and Christians can now approach each other as peer communities who have gained and abused power. The Church and the Synagogue need to be aware of their respective failings. Today Jews and Christians do not meet as victim and victimizer, but as two historical groups with experience of the exercise of power. In their encounter both faiths need to engage in a quest to strengthen their mutual traditions against false messianism. Such a development calls for a Jewish recovery of its prophetic voice. The Jewish community must develop solidarity with the poor and despised, including Jewish women, oriental Jews in Israel, and the Palestinian people. In this quest Christians must stand together with those Jews who are dedicated to those at the margin of society.

According to Reuther, this liberation theology of Christian-Jewish solidarity should meet on the mutual ground of a critique of false messianism. Traditionally, Jews regarded the claim that Jesus is the Messiah as a false messianism. Such a rejection implicitly assumes that the world is as yet unredeemed. Recently Christians have remodelled Christology accordingly. Jesus is hence viewed as a messianic prophet rather than the fulfilment of Jewish messianic hopes. Such a Christology coincides with the Jewish belief in the need to bring about God's Kingdom on earth. Thus, such a reinterpretation of Jesus' role as one who denounces oppression and injustice can draw Jews and Christians together in a common quest to bring about a better world. This critique of false-messianism can hence become an ideal for both peoples, involving a renewal of prophetic mission. As Reuther explains:

> Jews and Christians stand today not as particular to universal, and not simply as powerless to powerful, but as two historical communities, each with their histories of power and power-lessness, each with their hopes and their realities of failures . . . The unity of the planet points toward a One God, the source of all the world, the parent of all nations, not in the sense of demanding that all nations convert to one religion, but in the sense of making us siblings in one human family. Our source and goal in this one earth, and its God, calls us to end our sibling rivalry and realize our solidarity as a family of many peoples who must together become caretakers of one earth (Reuther, 1991, 93).

A Critical Perspective

In his contribution to *Judaism, Christianity and Liberation Theology*, the Jewish theologian Richard Rubenstein offers a critique of a Jewish theology of liberation. According to Rubenstein, Ellis has presented a theological and political assessment of Israel and the American Jewish community which is far harsher and more unrealistic than that proposed by the vast majority of Jewish intellectuals on the left. Ellis maintains that the dialectic of slavery and liberation is at the centre of Jewish life – in the modern world this vision has been betrayed by other interests and concerns. For Rubenstein, the charge of betrayal is insensitive to Jewish feelings as well as a misreading of history. For this reason Rubenstein believes that Ellis's *Toward a Jewish Theology of Liberation* is not likely to initiate a dialogue on a new Jewish theology:

> No matter what the shortcomings of the Jewish community, no theological writing will receive a serious hearing that repeats, albeit unintentionally, the kind of anti-Jewish defa-

mations that in the past have led to the casting of Jews wholly outside any shared universe of moral obligation with their neighbours (Rubenstein, 1991, 97).

No doubt Ellis would not support anti-Semitic defamations of the Jewish people, yet his remarks evoke subliminal stereotypes of Jews as deceitful and treacherous. Similarly Rubenstein argues that the New Testament portrayal of Jesus' condemnation of the leaders of the Jewish nation – a central element in my presentation in my book *On Earth as it is in Heaven* of the common ground between Jewish and Christian liberation theology – reinforces the negative image of the Jew. Such a depiction cannot, he believes, serve as a basis for theological encounter. Rather, fruitful theological exchange between Jews and Christians requires a re-evaluation of the charges levelled against the Jewish community in New Testament sources. Rubenstein writes:

> [The Gospels] cannot be taken uncritically as historical docu-ments; they must be seen, at least by theologians, in the light of the religious and political imperatives of the communities in which they arose (Rubenstein, 1991, 99).

Turning to Ellis's discussion of the conflict between Jews and the American black community, Rubenstein maintains that Ellis has distorted the nature of these events. There are, Rubenstein asserts, a number of important issues dividing Jewish conservatives and the mainstream black leadership in the USA. For example, the issue of affirm-ative action is one where blacks and Jewish conservatives adopt different ideological positions. Most Jews support the strict adherence to the merit system in university admis-sions and employment, regarding positive discrimination as unjust. Conversely the majority of blacks believe that the black community has suffered racial discrimination and has been denied equality in American society. Hence deeply-held opinions are in conflict – this is not simply the case of a Jewish betrayal of the prophetic dimensions of the faith.

Rubenstein is also highly critical of Ellis's allegation about the activities of Jews in Israel and North America.

According to Ellis, Israelis have oppressed Palestinians living in the West Bank and Gaza and have given assistance to murderous governments in Guatemala and El Salvador; in addition, Jewish neo-conservatives in America have abandoned Jewish ideals. Thus such figures as Greenberg are castigated for championing Jewish survival at the expense of other values. According to Greenberg, Israel's present experience of power should not be subjected to the standards of the ancient prophets – only those who are powerless can judge political action in terms of absolute principles. In place of such absolutes, Greenberg advocates a pragmatic approach which inevitably involves the occasional use of immoral strategies to achieve moral ends. For Ellis, such attitudes are abhorrent. To support this stance, Ellis cites the judgements of such writers as Earl Shorris and Roberta Strauss Feuerlicht; these figures, he argues, are the latter day prophets of the Jewish community. In addition, Ellis refers to the movements of Jewish renewal as signs of hope in a fallen world.

In response to this analysis of contemporary Jewish neo-conservatism, Rubenstein maintains that Ellis's account is one-sided. As far as Israeli politics is concerned, Ellis omits to say that the Arab States (except for Egypt) have refused to make peace with the Jewish State. Rather they have sought to delegitimize Israel and have fostered virulent anti-Semitism. Nor does Ellis mention that the West Bank was occupied because Jordan went to war against Israel in 1967 and was defeated. Although Israel's policy towards the Palestinians has its faults, the real problem is that the Palestinians see themselves as part of the Arab world that will some day eliminate the Jewish nation. Rubenstein writes:

> It is one thing for Israel to give up territory to an enemy who is willing to enter into a credible peace treaty. It is an altogether different matter to give up a territorial buffer to enemies bent on destruction (Rubenstein, 1991, 105).

According to Rubenstein, in formulating his Utopian programme of liberation Ellis has failed to recognize that in a world of conflict between peoples with opposing claims, it is simply impossible to make certain that everyone's rights will be ensured. In Rubenstein's opinion, a genuinely Jewish liberation theology must take greater account of the realities of contemporary life. As with a non-Utopian Christian theology, it should work for the betterment of those who are marginalized:

> It would do so by soundly-based economic and political measures that take full account of the modernizing economic and technological forces that have fostered mass marginalization since the beginnings of the industrial revolution. It would under no circumstances seek an overturning of the current economic and political order, which would inevitably end in tyranny, mass repression, and mass murder by regimes far more inhumane that the present bourgeois or rightwing governments, as the history of both the Soviet Union and the People's Republic of China demonstrate (Rubenstein, 1991, 108).

Theology after Auschwitz

In her contribution to *Judaism, Christianity and Liberation*, the German theologian Dorothee Sölle discusses Elie Wiesel's play, *The Trial of God*, which is set in Russia at the time of the Chmielnicki pogrom. In this dramatic presentation – which takes place in a small village inn at Schamgorod – God is accused of allowing children to suffer. Defending God against such a charge, a stranger named Sam protests: 'I am his servant. He created the world and us without seeking our opinion. He can act as he pleases. Our task is to glorify him notwithstanding' (Wiesel, 1977, 75). At the end of the play, it is revealed that Sam is in fact Satan. Commenting on this work Sölle emphasizes that Wiesel has posed the central dilemma of the Holocaust: how could God have allowed six million of his chosen people to die in the Nazi onslaught?

For Christians, Sölle argues, the Holocaust has profound religious significance and leads to a critical reading of the New Testament, a reinterpretation of church history, and a re-evaluation of Christology. In a post-Holocaust world, traditional theological solutions to the problem of theodicy must be superseded by the notion of a suffering Godhead. The question is not, 'how can God permit human suffering?' but, 'how does our pain become God's pain and how does God's pain appear in our pain? When the problem of suffering is formulated in this way, we are no longer bound to regard God in masculine terms. Rather:

> God is then our mother who cries about what we do to each other and about what we brothers and sisters do to animals and plants. God consoles us as a mother does, she cannot wave away pain magically . . . but she holds us on her lap, sometimes until we stand up again, our strength renewed, sometimes in a darkness without light . . . God cannot comfort us if she were not bound to us in pain, if she did not have this wonderful and exceptional ability to feel the pain of another in her own body, suffering with us, existing with us (Sölle, 1991, 114).

According to Sölle, the notion of God's enduring pain is rooted in the Christian tradition. In the New Testament Jesus is depicted as suffering. Thus if someone's face is slapped in his presence he feels the pain; when the whole nation is suppressed under the brutal force of imperialism, he weeps over Jerusalem. Again, in Paul's letters God is depicted as pained when he observes a barbaric world filled with injustice and the destruction of life. To participate in God's pain, Sölle argues, is to empathize with his grief. Thus in the gospel of John, Mary Magdalene, in refusing to be consoled over Jesus' death, is immersed in divine pain. As Sölle writes:

> Mary Magdalene does not accuse God, she does not defend God, she weeps; she is too deep in God to allow accusation or self-defense. Accusation would have required distance from God and she would have run away like the male disciples. But she is in God's pain (Sölle, 1991, 116).

To illustrate this thesis concerning God's pain, Sölle describes a visit she made to El Salvador. In this country, she writes, the poor are oppressed: they weep when their crops are burnt and when their teachers and trade union leaders are taken away and disappear. There she learned that the pain of the poor is also the pain of God. For Sölle, by suffering with the victims, God is able to transform their pain and deliver them. In the Hebrew Scriptures such a notion is eloquently expressed in Deutero-Isaiah:

> For a long time I have kept my peace. I have kept still and restrained myself; now I will cry out like a woman in travail . . . And I will lead the blind in a way that they know not, in paths that they have not known I will guide them. I will turn the darkness before them into light and the rough places into level ground. These are the things I will do and I will not forsake them (Isa. 42:14, 16).

Turning to the New Testament, Sölle cites John 16:

> You will be sorrowful, but your sorrow will turn into joy. When a woman is in travail, she has sorrow, beçause her hour has come; but when she is delivered of the child, she no longer remembers the anguish, for joy that a child is born into the world. So you have sorrow now, but I will see you again and your hearts will rejoice and no one will take your joy from you (John 16:20b–22).

But how does this transformation take place? To answer this question Sölle recounts an incident that took place one night in Manhattan. A beggar was squatting on a bundle of rags. When she gave him something, he raised his head, looked at her, and said, 'God bless you.' As time passed Sölle came to see that God's pain was manifest in this person's pain. In the presence of this beggar, Sölle's pain changed to anger, and she was engulfed by revulsion for a world that values uncontrolled economic growth. Her entire effort is now directed toward transforming her grief. 'The grief in which we live today,' she writes, 'becomes a uniting, warring, steadfast strength. My strength grows from my grief' (Sölle, 1991, 118).

For Sölle what is required today is a transformation of theological concern. Instead of attempting to reconcile the existence of evil with God's omnipotence, religious thinkers should strive to perceive God's pain in a post-Holocaust world. The recognition of God's self-limitation is the precondition of a new theology for the modern age. This perception of God's pain should lead to the quest to eradicate all injustice and suffering. Thus Sölle concludes:

> If we insist on just action and know that God 'has showed you, O man, what is good; and what does the Lord require of you but to do justice, and to love kindness, and to walk humbly with your God?' (Micah 6:8), then we can no longer separate theology and ethics. The Holocaust of the Jews calls us to resist the nuclear holocaust made possible by the excessive accumulation of arms, and waging war against today's and tomorrow's mass murder of the children of debtor nations. Then we will understand God in privation, growth, and suffering in the process of deliverance, which surpasses our wishes and fears, and calls us to participate in God's being (Sölle, 1991, 120).

Liberation Theology and Economics

In his discussion in *Judaism, Christianity and Liberation*, the Jewish scholar Norman Solomon outlines a number of reservations about a Jewish theology of liberation. First, Solomon questions the extent to which theologians should feel a duty to comment on social and economic matters. To illustrate this point he cites a story told about an autocratic Lithuanian rabbi in the early part of this century. In the course of his studies this scholar came across a detailed description of bricklaying by a medieval sage. On the basis of this account, he ordered the builders of the town to construct a building in accord with this sage's instructions. Not surprisingly the building collapsed. The point of this story is that although the rabbi was well-intentioned, he was misguided to interfere in affairs beyond his competence. Similarly Solomon believes that theologians must be careful not to make judgements about technical matters outside their sphere of expertise. In this connection, Solomon outlines several questions he believes should be asked about those liberationists who advance socio-economic schemes:

1. What are the ultimate economic aims formulated for society by theologians of liberation?
2. Granted that liberation theologians are justified in their complaints about economic exploitation in Latin America and elsewhere, does it follow that 'the [economic] system' as such is not the best available?
3. If 'the system' is not the best available, what alternative is proposed in its place?
4. Can theology decide between competing claims of different economic systems to achieve the ultimate aims the theologians have formulated? (Solomon, 1991, 124).

Solomon notes that in the writings of liberation theologians – who assert that their praxis is more important than theology – economic issues are generally not at the forefront; rather they tend to focus on such topics as 'liberation and salvation' and 'eschatology and politics'. None the less, liberationists do make statements of an economic character: frequently they use Marxist terminology and speak about a preferential option for the poor. Although Solomon admires the dedication and personal sacrifices of many of these writers, he is suspicious of their economic solutions. Thus he writes:

> The question addressed by this essay is not whether the basic communities are symbols of hope and light for our times, but whether they, or the theology of liberation in general, constitute the most effective response to the maldistribution of wealth, or to the other major issues they seek to highlight. It may well be that theologians, or prophets, are not the right people to solve such problems, even if they are an appropriate group to demand a solution (Solomon, 1991, 125).

Solomon is also sceptical of the extent to which the biblical model of the Exodus corresponds to the condition of the poor in Latin America. In Egypt the Hebrew slaves were oppressed, but through Moses' intervention they were freed from bondage. Although there are some parallels with the South American situation, important differences exist. In Egypt the Israelites were a minority, unlike those who are exploited in Latin America. In addition, they were foreigners; hence unlike the South American poor, they did not have the experience of being persecuted by their fellow countrymen. In addition, their liberation had nothing to do with poverty – rather it was a reminder of their identity as descendants of Abraham, Isaac and Jacob to whom God had promised he would grant a land of their own. Further, at Mount Sinai God revealed legislation needed for Israelite society. The Torah was proclaimed by God; it did not emerge from the basic community of the Israelites. Finally it should be noted that the Hebrews did very little to bring about their liberation; rather it was God who brought them out of the house of bondage. For all these reasons, Solomon contends that the story of Egyptian bondage does not offer a general paradigm for a critique of the causes of poverty.

Solomon also takes issue with the liberationists' concept of a 'preferential option for the poor.' As far as Judaism is concerned, the law dwells on the plight of those who are impoverished. Thus the Talmud states: 'Take care with the children of the poor – it is from them that Torah shall come forth to Israel.' None the less Solomon contends that since social reality is multifaceted, it should not be regarded exclusively from the perspective of one group. Although it is worthwhile to appreciate the perspective of those who are at the bottom, this is only one view among many. In this regard, Solomon is also critical of the idea that God shows favour to the poor:

> Surely God shows favour to those who love God and obey God's commandments, irrespective of whether they are rich or poor. God's 'principle', if so we may put it, is to help those in need, those who suffer oppression . . . God's Torah is universal, and does not favour one social stratum over another (Solomon, 1991, 130).

Finally, Solomon is concerned about the liberationists' espousal of Marxism. According to a number of liberation theologians, capitalism must be changed because it is a 'structure of sin'. Solomon, however, argues that 'a structure of sin' is not a particular type of socio-economic system, but a socio-economic system in which attitudes are motivated by greed and lust. What the Marxist analysis overlooks is the human propensity to sin. Socialist societies are no more free from greed, envy, corruption, or other human evils than capitalist societies. All socio-economic systems are subject to human sinfulness. By calling for a radical revision of the social order liberationists have inadvertently advocated the destabilization of society, and have thereby provided an opportunity for the unscrupulous to take charge. Moreover, they have discouraged constructive criticism of the existing system and have generated false hopes:

> The way ahead lies not in the revolutionary substitution of novel socio-economic systems for the present ones, but in the difficult and painstaking evolutionary process of curbing abuses that arise within the system (Solomon, 1991, 134).

4 Building Blocks of a Jewish Liberation Theology

As we have seen, there has been considerable interest within both the Jewish and the Christian communities regarding the development of a Jewish theology of liberation. The publication of my book, *On Earth as it is in Heaven: Jews, Christians and Liberation Theology* and Marc Ellis's book, *Toward a Jewish Theology of Liberation* has stimulated discussion in Jewish and Christian circles. Despite the reservations of such Jewish scholars as Judd Kruger Levingston, Richard Rubenstein and Norman Solomon, our advocacy of Jewish liberation theology has encouraged such writers as Leonardo Boff, Pablo Richard, Julio de Santa Ana, Michael Lerner, Rosemary Radford Reuther, and Dorothee Sölle to advance the project of a Jewish liberation theology. In different ways these writers have drawn attention to such issues as the State of Israel, the Palestinian question, the meaning of the Holocaust, the legacy of anti-Semitism, and the problem of empowerment. Such responses are an encouraging sign for those of us who have aligned themselves with this new theological development and have encouraged co-operation between Jews and Christians. What is now required is for Jews to focus on those features of their own faith which can be employed in formulating a Jewish theology of liberation which will confront the problems of the modern world.

Exodus and Freedom

A primary element of a contemporary Jewish theology of liberation is the celebration of freedom. Jews are all to rejoice in God's liberation of their ancestors, in which each of them takes part. Throughout the history of the Jewish people this festival has awakened the spirit of the people to the significance of human liberation. The biblical account of the Exodus, embodied in the liturgy of the Haggadah, has played a central role in the Jewish quest for human dignity and freedom. When we turn to the Passover in post-biblical literature, we find that Jewish writers saw in the Exodus a source of hope and inspiration, even during the darkest hours of Jewish history. The lessons of the Haggadah were taught repeatedly by Jewish sages in the Midrash and Talmud through commentary, interpretation, and legend; in this way new meanings were added to the biblical account.

In Midrash Shemot Rabbah, for example, the rabbis explained why Moses was chosen to lead the Hebrews out of Egypt:

> Our rabbis said that when Moses our teacher, peace be upon him, was tending the flock of Jethro in the wilderness, a little kid escaped from him. He ran after it until it reached a shady place. When it reached the shady place, there appeared to view a pool of water and the kid stopped to drink. When Moses approached it, he said: 'I did not know that you ran away because of thirst; you must be weary.' So he placed the kid on his shoulder and walked away. Thereupon God said, 'Because you have mercy in leading the flock of an animal, you will assuredly tend my flock Israel' [Midrash Shemot Rabbah 2.2].

In the Pirke de Rabbi Eliezer, the rabbis emphasized the symbolic significance of the burning bush. Commenting on Exodus 3:2, they asked why God showed Moses a bush burning with fire. The reason, they maintained, was because Moses had thought to himself that the Egyptians might consume Israel; hence God showed him a fire that burnt but did not consume, saying to him. 'Just as the thorn-bush is burning and is not consumed, so the Egyptians will not be able to destroy Israel' (Pirke de Rabbi Eliezer, 40).

Similarly, when Moses asked God for a sign, the Lord told him to cast his staff to the ground, and it became a fiery serpent. This was done to illustrate that as the serpent bites and kills human beings, so Pharaoh and his people bit and slew the Israelites (Pirke de Rabbi Eliezer, 40). Moses' hand became leprous in order to show that as the leper is unclean and causes uncleanliness, so Pharaoh and his people were unclean and they caused Israel to be unclean. Later however, Moses became clean again and God declared: 'Likewise Israel shall become clean from the uncleanliness of the Egyptians' (Pirke de Rabbi Eliezer, 40).

The rabbis emphasized that the God of the Israelites, unlike the gods of other nations, was the God of the living not the God of the dead. Thus, when Moses and Aaron stood before Pharaoh, they said to him: 'We are the ambassadors of the Lord.' When he heard their request, Pharaoh became very angry and said: 'Who is the Lord that I should hearken unto his voice to let Israel go? I know not the Lord, and moreover I will not let Israel go' (Exod. 5:2). He then went into his palace chamber and scrutinized every nation and its gods. He then said to them, 'I have searched for His name throughout my archives, but have not found him.' Moses and Aaron then said to Pharaoh, 'Idiot! Is it the way of the dead to be sought for among the living, or are the living among the dead? Our God is living, whereas those you mentioned are dead' (Midrash Shemot Rabbah 4.14).

The rabbis were anxious to point out that God was not responsible for Pharaoh's actions even though Scripture stated that God hardened Pharaoh's heart (Exod. 10:1). Simon b. Lakish declared:

> Let the mouths of the heretics be stopped up . . . When God warns a man once, twice, and even a third time, and he still does not repent, then does God close his heart against repentance so that He should exact vengeance from him for his sins. Thus it was with the wicked Pharaoh. Since God sent five times to him and he took no notice, God then said, 'You have stiffened your neck and hardened your heart; well, I will add to your uncleanliness!' (Midrash Shemot Rabbah 13.3).

Yet, despite this action, the rabbis emphasized that God does not rejoice in the downfall of the wicked. R. Johanan asks:

> What is the meaning of the verse, 'And one came not near the other all the night' (Exod. 14:20)? The ministering angels wanted to chant their hymns, but the Holy One, blessed be He, said, 'The work of my hands is being drowned in the sea, and shall you chant hymns?' (Megillah 10b).

Passover and Liberation

A second dimension of a Jewish liberation theology is the celebration of human freedom at Passover. Just as the rabbinic sources of the Tannaitic and Amoraic periods frequently alluded to the Exodus event as central in the life of the Jewish people, so too in Jewish literature of the medieval period were there frequent references to this act of deliverance commemorated in the Passover liturgy. Judah Halevi explains why the liturgy stated that the prohibition of work on the Sabbath and on Passover was a remembrance of the departure from Egypt. These two things belonged together, he wrote, because they were the outcome of the absolute divine will. Quoting Deuteronomy 4:32–34, he asserted:

> For ask now of the days past . . . whether there hath been any such things as this great thing, or hath been heard like it? Did ever people hear the voice of God speaking out of the midst of the fire, as thou hast heard, and live? Or hath God assayed to go and take Him a nation from the midst of another nation, by trials, by signs, and by wonders, and by war, and by a mighty hand, and by an outstretched arm, and by great terrors, according to all that the Lord your God did for you in Egypt before thine eyes? (Halevi (1927) 1964, 114).

Saadia Gaon in *The Book of Doctrines and Beliefs* argued that the redemption from bondage was inevitable. God, he maintained, was just and would not do wrong. Having inflicted on the Jewish people prolonged suffering as a punishment, God set a time limit to their affliction. 'Bid

Jerusalem take heart and proclaim unto her that her time of service is accomplished, that her guilt is paid off, that she hath received of the Lord's hand double for all her sins' (Isa. 40:2).

Furthermore, God was a faithful keeper of promises; thus the promise that God would mete out judgment to the oppressors of the Jews and reward the Hebrew nation was certain to be fulfilled: 'And also that nation whom they shall serve, will I judge; and afterwards, they shall come out with great substance' (Gen. 15:14). For the trials of the past God would give the people a double of its double share – over and above what had been promised. Thus it was said: 'And He will do thee good and multiply thee above thy fathers' (Deut. 30:5). For this reason Saadia asserted:

> He mentions to us the Exodus from Egypt so frequently and in so many places. He wants us to remember the things we experienced. If anything which He did for use in the course of the redemption from Egypt is not explicitly included in the promise of the final Redemption, it is implied in the statement, 'As in the days of thy coming forth out of the land of Egypt, will I show unto him marvellous things' (Micah 7:15) (Gaon, 1946, 168–9).

The Zohar, the medieval mystical book, relates that the joy of the Passover caused God to rejoice and call together all the heavenly hosts and say to them:

> 'Come ye and hearken unto the praises which my children bring unto me. Behold how they rejoice in redemption!' Then all the angels gathered together and observed Israel's singing because of God's redemption. Seeing this they also broke into rejoicing that God possessed such a people whose joy in the redemption was so great and powerful. For all that terrestrial rejoicing increased the power of the Lord and His hosts in the regions above, just as an earthly king gained strength from the praises of his subjects, the fame of his glory being thus spread throughout the world (Zohar, 'Ray'a Mehamna', BO, 40b).

Modern Jewish writers of post-Enlightenment Judaism

similarly emphasized the significance of the themes of liberty, redemption, and freedom as found in the Passover festival. Franz Rosenzweig, for example, argued that there was an intrinsic connection between the Passover and the Sabbath. The Sabbath, he maintained, is a reminder of the Exodus from Egypt:

> The freedom of the man-servant and the maid-servant which it proclaims is conditioned by the deliverance of the people as a people from the servitude of Egypt. And in every command to respect the freedom of even the man-servant, of even the alien among the people, the law of God renews the awareness of the connection holding between the freedom within the people, a freedom decreed by God, and the freeing of the people from Egyptian servitude, a liberation enacted by God (Rosenzweig, 1953, 319–21).

The Passover meal was a symbol of Israel's vocation as a people; the deliverance of the nation afforded a glimpse of its destiny. It was not only then that enemies rose up against the Jews; enemies have arisen in every generation, and God has always taken the side of the chosen people. All this pointed to the ultimate redemption as prophesied by Isaiah – of the day when the wolf would dwell with the lamb and the world would be as full of the knowledge of the Lord as the sea is of water (Rosenzweig, 1953, 319–21).

The moral implications of the redemption from Egypt were emphasized by M. Lazarus in *The Ethics of Judaism*. The Exodus, he wrote, had a predominant place in the biblical and rabbinic cycle of religious ideas. The most exalted moral statutes in the Torah concerning the treatment of strangers were connected with the Exodus, and were, from a psychological point of view, impressively elucidated by means of the injunction: 'Ye know the heart of the stranger' (Exod. 23:9). The prophets and the psalmists used this event to illustrate God's providence and grace, and the rabbis deduced from it the two fundamental aspects of Jewish ethics: the notion of liberty and the ethical task of humankind. Lazarus remarked that, throughout the history of Judaism:

the notion of liberty, inner moral and spiritual liberty, cherished as a pure, exalted ideal, possible only under and through the Law, was associated with the memory of the redemption from Egyptian slavery, and this memory in turn was connected with symbolic practices accompanying every act, pleasure, and celebration (Lazarus, 1900, 28–9, 231–2).

Kaufman Kohler saw in the Passover a symbol of thanksgiving and hope that sustained the Jewish nation in its tribulations:

> The Passover festival with its 'night of divine watching' endowed the Jew ever anew with endurance during the dark night of medieval tyranny and with faith in 'the Keeper of Israel who slumbereth not nor sleepeth' (Kohler, 1968, 462).

Moreover, he believed that the feast of redemption promised a day of liberty to those who continued to struggle under oppression and exploitation:

> The modern Jew is beginning to see in the reawakening of his religious and social life in Western lands the token of the future liberation of all mankind. The Passover feast brings him the clear and hopeful message of freedom for humanity from all bondage of today and of spirit (Kholer, 1968, 462).

Morris Joseph also focused on the contemporary significance of Passover (*Judaism as Creed and Life*). It is, he believed, the greatest of all the historical festivals in that it brings the Jews into close contact with the past. No other festival, he contended, so powerfully appeals to historical sympathies. At the Passover ceremony the Jews are at one with their redeemed ancestors; they share with the ancestors the consciousness of freedom, the sense of nationality that was beginning to stir in their hearts. 'He [the Jew] shares,' Joseph wrote, 'their glowing hopes, the sweet joy of newly recovered manhood' (Joseph, 1903, 213–15).

Through God's redemption, the Israelites were able to free themselves from despair, and all Jews, past and present, share in this deliverance.

We march forth with them from the scenes of oppression in

gladness and gratitude. The ideal of the rabbis fulfils itself. 'In every generation it is for the Jew to think that he himself went forth from Egypt' (Pesahim 10:5) (Joseph, 1903, 213–15).

Ahad Ha-Am concentrated on Moses the Liberator as an ideal type of hero. Moses, he pointed out, was neither a warrior nor a statesman. He was a prophet, who put justice into action. Confronted with acts of iniquity, he took the side of the victim. The events of his early life, when he struggled against injustice, served as a prelude to his revolt against Egyptian oppression:

> That great moment dawned in the wilderness, far from the turmoil of life. The prophet's soul is weary of the endless struggle, and longs for peace and rest. He seeks the solitude of the shepherd's life, goes into the wilderness with his sheep, and reaches Horeb, the mountain of the Lord. But even here he finds no rest. He feels in his innermost being that he has not yet fulfilled his mission . . . Suddenly the prophet hears the voice of the Lord – the voice he knows so well – calling to him from some forgotten corner of his innermost being: 'I am the God of thy father . . . I have surely seen the affliction of My people that are in Egypt . . . Come now therefore, and I will send thee unto Pharaoh, that thou mayest bring forth My people the children of Israel out of Egypt!' (Ahad Ha-Am, 1946, 103–8).

The Prophetic Tradition

Another feature of a Jewish theology of liberation is the prophetic tradition. The earliest Hebrew prophet, whose book was dedicated to the proclamation of God's ethical requirements, was Amos, a shepherd from Tekoa who was active around 760 BC. As in Jesus' day, then too the rich oppressed the poor, bribed judges in court, and cheated one another with false weights and measures. The religion of God, which had stressed the social justice of covenant law, had declined in importance and was thwarted by the king's syncretistic tendencies. In this atmosphere Amos railed against the people. Israel had sinned, he declared,

because they sell the righteous for silver,
and the needy for a pair of shoes –
they that trample the head of the poor
into the dust of the earth
and turn aside the way of the afflicted;
a man and his father go in to the same maiden,
so that my holy name is profaned;
they lay themselves down beside every altar
upon garments taken in pledge;
and in the house of their God they drink
the wine of those who have been fined (Amos 2:6–8).

Amos reacted to what he saw: the rich exploited the poor;
women were used immorally; legal pledges were treated
sacrilegiously. Amos emphasized that observing ritual
would do no good as long as the Israelites continued to
sin. Speaking in God's name, he declared:

I hate, I despise your feasts,
and I take no delight in your solemn assemblies.
Even though you offer me your burnt offerings and cereal
offerings,
I will not accept them,
and the peace offerings of your fatted beasts
I will not look upon.
Take away from me the noise of your songs;
to the melody of your harps I will not listen.
But let justice roll down like waters,
and righteousness like an overflowing stream (Amos 5:21–24).

Though some commentators have interpreted this passage
as a condemnation of every type of cultic practice, it is
more likely that Amos was here decreeing that cultic sacrifice by itself was not what God required; it must be
accompanied by a dedication to righteousness and justice.
Amos continued his diatribe against unrighteousness by
condemning luxury:

Woe to those who lie upon beds of ivory,
and stretch themselves upon their couches,
and eat lambs from the flock,
and calves from the midst of the stall;
who sing idle songs to the sound of the harp,

and like David invent for themselves instruments of music;
who drink wine in bowls
and anoint themselves with the finest oils (6:4–6).

In the midst of such self-indulgence, the rich remained unconcerned with the plight of the poor:

Hear this word, you cows of Bashan,
who are in the mountain of Samaria
who oppress the poor, who crush the needy,
who say to their husbands,
'Bring, that we may drink!' (4:1–2).

Such indifference, he declared, condemned those who luxuriated in their wealth:

O you who turn justice to wormwood,
and cast down righteousness to the earth! . . .
Therefore because you trample upon the poor
and take from him exactions of wheat . . .
For I know how many are your transgressions,
and how great are your sins –
you who afflict the righteous, who take a bribe
and turn aside the needy in the gate (5:7, 11–12).

The merchants too were rebuked; they observed the holy days, but exploited the poor in the markets:

Hear this, you who trample upon the needy,
and bring the poor of the land to an end,
saying, 'When will the new moon be over,
that we may sell grain?
And the sabbath,
that we may offer wheat for sale,
that we may make the ephah small and the shekel great,
and deal deceitfully with false balances,
that we may buy the poor for silver
and the needy for a pair of sandals,
and sell the refuse of the wheat?' (8:4–6).

Several decades after Amos began his ministry in Israel, Isaiah began his prophetic mission in Judah. God had chosen Israel to produce justice, Isaiah proclaimed, but instead it created bloodshed (Isa. 5:7). Like Amos, Isaiah protested against the indifference of the rich to the poor and oppressed:

It is you who have devoured the vineyard,
the spoil of the poor is in your houses.
What do you mean by crushing my people,
by grinding the face of the poor? (3:14–15).

Isaiah condemned the offering of sacrifice without an accompanying quest for righteousness. Paralleling the message of Amos, he declared:

What to me is the multitude of your sacrifices?
says the Lord;
I have had enough of burnt offering of rams
and the fat of fed beasts;
I do not delight in the blood of bulls,
or of lambs, or of he-goats.
When you come to appear before me,
who requires of you
this trampling of my courts?
Bring no more vain offerings;
incense is an abomination to me.
New moon and sabbath and the calling of assemblies –
I cannot endure iniquity and solemn assembly . . .
Wash yourselves; make yourselves clean;
remove the evil of your doings from before my eyes;
cease to do evil, learn to do good;
seek justice, correct oppression;
defend the fatherless, plead for the widow (1:11–13, 16–17).

According to Isaiah, Israel was a sinful nation – a band of wrongdoers (1:4); the nation had turned away from God. Thus he condemned the women of Jerusalem who arrogantly and wantonly strolled through the streets (3:16–24), the priests and false prophets who drunkenly proclaimed their messages (28:7–13), and the judges who issued tyrannical judgments, cheated the poor, widows, and orphans, and grew wealthy on bribes (10:1–4).

The religious reforms of Hezekiah (715–687 BC) were overturned by Manasseh (687–642 BC) who reinstated Assyrian astral deities and Canaanite fertility gods. This was subsequently attacked by Josiah's radical religious reform (640–609 BC). It is possible that Jeremiah was involved in this recommitment to covenant Law, to the destruction of the sanctuaries in the high places, and to the centralization of the cult in the Jerusalem Temple. Like Amos and Isaiah, he emphasized that God demands righteousness from the people. In a sermon delivered in about 609 BC he insisted that it was wrong to assume that Jerusalem was immune from attack because God's presence in the Temple provided protection:

> Do not trust in these deceptive words: 'This is the temple, of the Lord, the temple of the Lord, the temple of the Lord . . .' Will you steal, murder, commit adultery, swear falsely, burn incense to Ba'al, and go after other gods that you have not known, and then come and stand before me in this house, which is called by my name, and say, 'We are delivered!' (Jer. 7:4, 9–10).

Religious practice was of no avail if human justice and devotion to God were neglected.

The Classical prophets, as well as the post-exilic prophets, who carried on and elaborated the message, became the conscience of the nation. They attacked the people's iniquity and the people's exploitation of the poor by the rich. God's covenant, they insisted, demanded compassion, justice, and righteousness.

The Kingdom of God

A further aspect of a Jewish theology of liberation is the concept of the Kingdom of God. God's kingdom is understood as intimately connected with the establishment of justice on earth. In the psalms, God is extolled as a king who judges justly. It was he who righted injustice; he was the heavenly king who established and maintained justice on earth:

> But the Lord sits enthroned for ever
> He has established his throne from judgment;
> he judges the world with righteousness;
> he judges the people with equity.

The Lord is a stronghold for the oppressed,
a stronghold in times of trouble.
And those who know thy name put their trust in thee,
for thou, O Lord, has not forsaken those who seek thee (Ps
9:7–10).

This motif of God as the king who rights the wrongs of
the world was related to the Israelite legal emphasis on the
rights of the orphan, the widow, and the resident foreigner.
According to Psalm 82 it is because the other so-called
gods do not right the wrongs of this world that they expose
themselves as unworthy!

God has taken his place in the divine council;
in the midst of the gods he holds judgment:
'How long will you judge unjustly
and show partiality to the wicked?
Give justice to the weak and the fatherless;
maintain the right of the afflicted and the destitute.
Rescue the weak and the needy;
deliver them from the hand of the wicked.'

They have neither knowledge nor understanding,
they walk about in darkness;
all the foundations of the earth are shaken.
I say, 'You are gods,
sons of the Most High, all of you;
nevertheless, you shall die like men,
and fall like any prince' (Ps 82:1–7)

God's nature was to be the divine king who acts justly,
and Israel was enjoined to be like God. The Lord stood
for righteousness and justice; so too must the earthly king
act with loving-kindness and equity:

Give the king thy justice, O God,
and thy righteousness to the royal son!
May he judge thy people with righteousness
and thy poor with justice!

Let the mountains bear prosperity for the people,
and the hills, in righteousness!
May he defend the cause of the poor of the people,
give deliverance to the needy,
and crush the oppressor! (Ps 72:1–4).

Ordinary citizens too were called to the justice of God. By keeping God's commandments Israel was to become truly God's child by bringing peace to earth. When the people acted unjustly, the psalmist called them to account:

> Hear, O my people, and I will speak,
> O Israel, I will testify against you.
> I am God, your God . . .
>
> What right have you to recite my statutes,
> or take my covenant on your lips?
> For you hate discipline,
> and you cast my words behind you.
>
> If you see a thief, you are a friend of his;
> and you keep company with adulterers.
> You give your mouth free rein for evil,
> and your tongue frames deceit.
> You sit and speak against your brother;
> you slander your own mother's son (Ps 50:7, 16–20).

Jewish Moral Principles

Another fundamental dimension of a Jewish theology of liberation is the ethical tradition within rabbinic sources. Moral precepts are grounded in the will of God; in this light the Torah serves as the blueprint for moral action, and it is through the admonitions of the rabbis in Midrashic and Talmudic sources that the Jewish people are encouraged to put the teachings of the Law into effect in their everyday life. In the hierarchy of values, the rabbis declared that justice is of fundamental importance. R. Simeon b. Gamliel, for example, remarked: 'Do not sneer at justice, for it is one of the three feet of the world, for the sages taught that the world stands on three things: justice, truth and peace' (Deut. R. Shofetim, V, 1 and 3). According to R. Elazar,

> the whole Torah depends upon justice. Therefore God gave enactments about justice (Exod. 21:10) immediately after the Ten Commandments, because men transgress justice, and God punishes them, and He teaches the inhabitants of the

world. Sodom was not overthrown till the men of Sodom neglected justice, and the men of Jerusalem were not banished till they disregarded justice (Ezek. 16:49; Isa. 1:23 (Ex. R. Mishpatim, 30, 19).

In explaining what was entailed in the principle of justice, the rabbis explained what was required in a court of law. With reference to the Deuteronomic injunction, 'thou shalt not take a bribe, for a bribe blinds the eyes of the wise' (Deut. 16:19), R. Hama b. Osha'ya stated:

> If a man suffers from his eyes, he pays much money to a doctor, but it is doubtful whether he will be healed or not. But he who takes a bribe, overturns justice, blinds his eyes, brings Israel into exile and hunger into the world (Tanh B., Shofetim, 15b fin.)

Regarding the statement, 'In righteousness shall thou judge thy neighbour' (Lev. 19:15), the Sifra proclaimed:

> You must not let one litigant speak as much as he wants, and then say to the other 'shorten thy speech'. You must not let one stand and the other sit (Sifra 89a).

Simeon b. Shetach said:

> When you are judging, and there come before you two men, of whom one is rich and the other poor, do not say, 'thy poor man's words are to be believed, but not the rich man's'. But just as you listen to the words of the poor man, listen to the words of the rich man, for it is said, 'Ye shall not respect persons in judgement' (Deut. 1:17) (Ab.R.N. (vers. II), XX, 22a).

Like justice, charity was viewed as an essential virtue. The Talmud declared: 'He who gives alms in secret is greater than Moses' (Bab. B. 9b). In another Talmudic passage R. Elazar stated:

> Almsgiving is greater than all sacrifice for it says, 'To give alms is more acceptable to God than sacrifices' (Prov. 21:3). But loving deeds are greater than almsgiving, as it says, 'Sow in almsgiving, reap in love' (Hos. 10:12). Of his sowing, a man may eat or no; of his reaping, he will eat assuredly. And

he said: 'Almsgiving becomes increasingly perfect according to the amount of love that is shown in it' (Suk. 49b).

According to the midrash on the psalms, the gates of the Lord were open to one who cared for others:

> In the future world, man will be asked, 'What was your occupation?' If he replies, 'I fed the hungry', then they reply, 'This is the gate of the Lord; he who feeds the hungry, let him enter' (Ps 118:20). So with giving drink to the thirsty, clothing to the naked, with those who look after orphans, and with those, generally, who do deeds of loving kindness. All these are gates of the Lord, and those who do such deeds shall enter within them (Midr. Ps., 118:19).

Hospitality was also considered a cardinal virtue. In a commentary on Exodus we read:

> God said to Moses, 'I will send thee to Pharaoh.' Moses answered, 'Lord of the world, I cannot; for Jethro has received me, and opened his house door to me, so that I am as a son with him. If a man opens his house to his fellow, his guest owes his life to him. Jethro has received me, and has honourably entertained me; can I depart without his leave?' Hence it says, 'Moses went and returned to Jethro his father-in-law' (Tanh, Shemot, §16, f87a).

Great is hospitality, the rabbi decreed, 'greater even than early attendance at the House of Study or than the reception of the Shekhinah [God's presence]' (Sab. 127a).

These few examples indicate that the Kingdom of God is inconsistent with injustice and social misery; the effort to bring about the perfection of the world so that God will reign in majesty is a human responsibility. Jewish ethics as enshrined in the Bible and in rabbinic literature was inextricably related to the coming of God's kingdom. In this context a number of distinctive characteristics of Jewish morality are expressed in the Jewish tradition.

First, as we have seen in connection with the prophets, there was an intensity of passion about the moral demands made upon human beings. For sins of personal greed, social inequity, and deceit, the prophet in God's name denounced the people and threatened horrific catastrophes. The voice of the prophet was continually charged with agony and agitation. Habbakuk, for example, declared:

> Woe to him who heaps up what is not his own . . .
> Woe to him who gets evil for his house . . .
> For the stone will cry out from the wall,
> And the beam from the woodwork respond.
> Woe to him who builds a town with blood,
> and founds a city on iniquity (Hab. 2:6, 9, 11–12).

Such shrill denunciations of iniquity were the result of the prophetic conviction that people must be stirred from their spiritual slumber. 'The prophet's word is a scream in the night . . . while the world is at ease and asleep, the prophet feels the blast from heaven' (Heschel, 1955, 16).

Second, Jewish ethics requires that each person be treated equally. Biblical and rabbinic sources show a constant concern to eliminate arbitrary distinctions between individuals so as to establish a proper balance between competing claims. On the basis of the biblical view that everyone is created in the image of God, the Torah declared that false and irrelevant distinctions must not be introduced to disqualify human beings from the right to justice. The fatherhood and motherhood of God implied human solidarity; the Torah rejected the idea of different codes of morality for oneself and others, for the great and the humble, for rulers and ruled, for individuals and nations, for private and public citizens. Given this understanding of the equality of all people, the Torah singled out the underprivileged and the defenceless in society for consideration: 'You shall not afflict any widow or fatherless child' (Exod. 22:22). 'Thou shalt not respect the person of the poor nor honour the person of the great' (Lev. 19:15).

Since all of humanity is created in the image of God, Judaism maintains that there is no fundamental difference between Jew and non-Jew: God's ethical demands apply to all. In the Midrash we read:

This is the gate of the Lord into which the righteous shall

enter: not priest, Levites, or Israelites, but the righteous, though they be non-Jews (Sifra, Acharei Mot, 13).

Indeed, according to the Talmud, the righteous non-Jew was accorded a place in the hereafter: 'The pious of all nations have a share in the world to come' (Sanhedrin 105a). In this light, the rabbis emphasized that Jews must treat their non-Jewish neighbours with loving-kindness. One of the most authoritative rabbis of the last century declared:

> It is well known that the early as well as the later geonim wrote that we must abide by the law of the land and refrain from dealing unjustly with a non-Jew . . . Therefore, my brethren, listen to my voice and live. Study in our Torah to love the Almighty and love people regardless of faith or nationality. Follow justice and do righteousness with Jew and non-Jew alike. The people of my community know that I always caution them in my talks and warn them that there is absolutely no difference whether one does evil to a Jew or a non-Jew. It is a well-known fact that when people come to me to settle a dispute, I do not differentiate between Jew and non-Jew. For that is the law according to our holy Torah (Spektor, 1983, 134).

A third characteristic of Jewish morality is its emphasis on human motivation. The Jewish faith is not solely concerned with actions and their consequences; it also demands right intention. The rabbis explained: 'The Merciful One requires the heart' (San. 106b). It is true that Judaism emphasizes the importance of moral action, but the Jewish faith also focuses attention on rightmindedness: inner experiences – motives, feelings, dispositions, and attitudes – are of supreme moral significance. For this reason the rabbis identified a group of negative commandments in the Torah involving thought. The following are representative examples:

> Thou shalt not take vengeance, nor bear any grudge against the children of thy people (Deut. 15:7).
> There are six things which the Lord hateth . . . a heart that deviseth wicked thoughts (Prov. 6:16, 18).

Beware that there be not a base thought in thy heart (Deut. 15:9).

In the Mishnah the rabbis elaborated on this concern for the human heart:

> Rabbi Eliezer said, ' . . . be not easily moved to anger' (Avot 2.15)
> Rabbi Joshua said, 'The evil eye, the evil inclination, and hatred of his fellow creatures drives a man out of the world' (Avot 2.16).
> Rabbi Levitas of Yavneh said, 'Be exceedingly lowly of spirit' (Avot 2.16).

Connected with right thought is the Jewish emphasis on right speech. Jewish sources insist that individuals are morally responsible for the words they utter. Proverbs declared: 'Death and life are in the power of the tongue' (18:21). Evil words spoken about one person by another could arouse hatred and enmity and destroy human relations. The rabbis considered slander to be a particular evil:

> Whoever speaks slander is as though he denied the fundamental principle (existence of God). The Holy One, blessed be He, says of such a person who speaks slander, 'I and he cannot dwell together in the world' (Pe'ah 15d, Areakh in 15b).

There was also a positive aspect to this emphasis on human speech. Just as the rabbis condemned false utterances, they urged their disciples to offer cheerful greetings (Avot 1.15, 3.16, 12). Anger could be soothed with gentle words and reconciliation could be brought about (Spero, 1983, 148).

A fourth dimension of Jewish morality concerns the traditional attitude towards animals. Since God's mercy and goodness extend to all creatures, 'a righteous man regardeth the life of the beast' (Ps 145:9; Prov. 12:10). According to Jewish tradition, human beings are morally obliged to refrain from inflicting pain on animals. The Pentateuch stipulated that assistance be given to animals in distress even on the Sabbath: 'Thou shalt not see thy brother's ass or his ox fallen down by the way and hide thyself from them; thou shalt surely help him to lift them up again'

(Deut. 22:4). In rabbinic Judaism, this same theme was reflected in various midrashim. We read, for example, concerning Rabbi Judah Ha-Nasi:

> Rabbi Judah was sitting and studying the Torah in front of the Babylonian synagogue in Sepphoris, when a calf passed before him on its way to the slaughter and began to cry out as though pleading, 'Save me!' Said he to it, 'What can I do for you? For this you were created.' As a punishment for his heartlessness, he suffered toothache for thirteen years. One day, a weasel ran past his daughter, who was about to kill it, when he said to her, 'My daughter, let it be, for it is written. "and His tender mercies are over all His works." ' Because the Rabbi prevented an act of cruelty, he was once again restored to health (Baba Metzia, 85a).

A final aspect of Jewish ethics is its concern for human dignity; Judaism puts a strong emphasis on the respect due to all individuals. This concept was found in various laws in the Pentateuch and was developed by the rabbis who cautioned that one must be careful not to humiliate or embarrass others. Maimonides, for example, wrote:

> A man ought to be especially heedful of his behaviour towards widows and orphans, for their souls are exceedingly depressed and their spirits low, even if they are wealthy. How are we to conduct ourselves toward them? One must not speak to them otherwise than tenderly. One must show them unvarying courtesy; not hurt them physically with hard toil nor wound their feelings with harsh speech (Hilchot De'ot 6.10).

The Torah's concern for human dignity even included thieves. Rabbi Yochanan ben Zakai pointed out that according to the Law whoever stole a sheep should pay a fine of four times the value of the sheep; whoever stole an ox must pay five times its value. Those who stole sheep had to undergo the embarrassment of carrying the sheep off in their arms and the Torah compensated them for this indignity, but those who stole oxen were spared such embarrassment because they could simply lead the ox by its tether (Baba Kamma 99b).

Judaism and Moral Action

A final dimension of a theology of liberation is the Jewish emphasis on moral action. For Jews history matters. The Jewish hope for the future lies in God's sovereign rule on earth. From ancient times the synagogue liturgy concluded with a prayer in which this hope was expressed:

> May we speedily behold the glory of Thy might,
> when Thou wilt remove the abominations from the earth,
> and the idols will be utterly cut off;
> when the world will be perfected under the kingdom of the Almighty,
> and all the children of flesh will call upon Thy name;
> when Thou wilt turn unto Thyself all the wicked of the earth.

This is the goal of the history of the world in which God's chosen people have a central role. In this context the people of Israel have a historical mission to be a light to the nations. Through Moses God addressed the people and declared:

> You have seen what I did to the Egyptians, and how I bore you on eagles' wings, and brought you unto myself. Now therefore, if you will obey my voice and keep my covenant, you shall be my own possession among all people; for all the earth is mine, and you shall be to me a kingdom of priests and a holy nation (Exod. 19:4-6).

Election was to be a servant of the Lord, to proclaim God's truth and righteousness throughout the world. Being chosen meant duty and responsibility; it was:

> a divine call persisting through all ages and encompassing all lands, a continuous activity of the spirit which has ever summoned for itself new heralds and heroes to testify to truth, justice and sublime faith (Kohler (1918) 1968, 326).

Judaism did not separate religion from life; instead Jews were called to action, to turn humankind away from violence, wickedness, and falsehood. It was not the hope of bliss in a future life but the establishment of the kingdom of justice and peace that was central to the Jewish faith. Moral praxis was at the heart of the religious tradition.

The people of Israel as a light to the nations reflected the moral nature of God; each Jew was to be like the creator, mirroring the divine qualities revealed to Moses:

> The Lord, the Lord, a God merciful and gracious, slow to anger, and abounding in steadfast love and faithfulness, keeping steadfast love for thousands, forgiving iniquity and transgression and sin (Exod. 34:6–7).

God as a moral being demanded moral living, as the Psalms declared: 'The Lord is righteous; He loves righteous deeds' (Ps 11–7). 'Righteousness and justice are the foundation of His throne' (Ps 97:2). 'Thou hast established equity; thou hast executed justice and righteousness' (Ps 99:4). Given this theological framework, Jews were directed to obey the revealed will of God, which was the basis of the covenantal relationship between God and the Jewish nation. Ortho-praxis, rather than conceptual reflection, served as the foundation of the religion of Israel.

In the Bible, deeds and events involving moral issues can be found in abundance: the punishment of Cain for murdering his brother, the violence of the generation that brought on the Flood, the early prohibition against murder, the hospitality of Abraham and his pleading for the people of Sodom, the praise of Abraham for his moral attitudes, the condemnation of Joseph's brothers, Joseph's self-restraint in the house of Potiphar, Moses' intercessions on the side of the exploited (Spero, 1983, 22).

But it is pre-eminently in the legal codes of the Pentateuch that we encounter moral guidelines formulated in specific rules. The Decalogue in particular illustrates the centrality of moral praxis in the life of the Jew. The first four commandments are theological in character, but the last six deal with relationships between human beings. The first commandment describes God as the one who redeemed the Jews from Egypt; the one who forbade the worship of other deities and demanded respect for the Sabbath and the divine name. These commandments were expressions of the love and fear of God; the remaining injunctions provided a means of expressing love of other human beings. The Decalogue made it clear that moral rules were fundamental to the Jewish faith.

Such ethical standards were repeated in the prophetic books. The teachings of the prophets were rooted in the Torah of Moses. The prophets saw themselves as messengers of the divine word; their special task was to denounce the people for their transgressions and call them to repentance. In all this they pointed to concrete action – moral praxis – as the only means of sustaining the covenantal relationship with God. The essential theme of their message was that God demanded righteousness and justice.

Emphasis on the moral life was reflected in the prophetic condemnation of cultic practices that were not accompanied by ethical concern. These passages illustrated that ritual commandments were of instrumental value; morality was intrinsic and absolute. The primacy of morality was also reflected in the prophetic warning that righteous action was the determining factor in the destiny of the Jewish nation. Moral transgressions referred to in such contexts concerned exploitation, oppression, and the perversion of justice. These sins had the potential to bring about the downfall of the nation.

The Book of Proverbs reinforced the teaching of the Torah and the prophets; wisdom was conceived here as a capacity to act morally; it was a skill that could be learned. Throughout Proverbs dispositional traits were catalogued: the positive moral types included the *tzaddik*, the *chakham*, and the *yashar*, the evil characters included the *rasha*, the *avil*, the *kheseil*, the *letz*, and the *peti*.

> This suggests that moral virtue or vice is to be achieved not by concentrating on individual moral acts but rather by learning to recognise and emulate certain good personality types (Spero, 1983, 42).

Thus here, as in the rest of the Bible, the moral life was seen as the foundation of the Jewish faith. Theology was defined in relation to practical activity; it was through ethical praxis that humanity encountered the Divine.

Rabbinic literature continued this emphasis on action.

Convinced they were the authentic expositors of Scripture, the rabbis amplified biblical law. In their expansion of the commandments, rabbinic exegetes differentiated between the laws governing human relationships to God *bain adam la makom* and those that concerned human relationships to others *bain adam le chavero*. As in the biblical period, rabbinic teachings reflected the same sense of the primacy of morality. Such texts as the following indicated rabbinic priority:

> He who acts honestly and is popular with his fellow creatures, it is imputed to him as though he had fulfilled the entire Torah.
> Hillel said: 'What is hateful to yourself, do not do to your fellow man.
> This is the entire Torah, the rest is commentary.'

> Better is one hour of repentance and good deeds in this world than the whole life of the world-to-come (Spero, 1983, 56–7).

In the classic texts of Judaism, then, moral behaviour was the predominant theme. By choosing the moral life, the Jew could help to complete God's work of creation. To accomplish this task the rabbis formulated an elaborate system of traditions, which were written down in the Mishnah, subsequently expanded in the Talmud, and eventually codified in the Code of Jewish Law. According to traditional Judaism, this expansion of the Pentateuchal Law was part of God's revelation. Both the Written Law (*Torah Shebik-thav*) and the Oral Law (*Torah Shebe-'alpe*) were binding on Jews for all time.

> The Torah has been revealed from Heaven. This implies our belief that the whole of the Torah found in our hands this day is the Torah that was handed down by Moses and that it is all of divine origin. By this I mean that the whole of the Torah came unto him from before God in a manner which is metaphorically called speaking (Maimonides, as quoted in Jacobs, 1964, 216).

This Torah embraced the Pentateuch as well as its traditional interpretation: orthodoxy maintained that God gave to Moses the laws in the Pentateuch as well as their explanations.

> The verse: 'And I will give thee the tables of stone, and the Law and the commandment, which I have written that thou mayest teach them' (Exod. 24:12) means as follows: 'The tables of stone' are the ten commandments; 'the law' is the Pentateuch; 'the commandment' is the Mishnah; 'which I have written' are the Prophets and the Hagiographa; 'that thou mayest teach them' is the Gemara (Talmud). This teaches that all these things were given on Sinai (R. Levi b. Hama in the name of R. Simeon b. Laquish, in Jacobs, 1964. 282).

Given this view of the Torah, Jews regarded the moral law as absolute and binding. In all cases the law was precise and specific; it was God's word made concrete in the daily life of the Jew. The commandment to love one's neighbours embraced all humanity. In the Code of Jewish Law the virtues of justice, honesty, and humane concern were regarded as central virtues of community life; hatred, vengeance, deceit, cruelty, and anger were condemned as anti-social. The Jew was instructed to exercise loving-kindness towards all: to clothe the naked, to feed the hungry, to care for the sick, and to comfort the mourner. By fulfilling these ethical demands, the Jewish people could help to bring about God's kingdom on earth, in which exploitation, oppression, and injustice would be eliminated. What was required in this task was a commitment to ethical praxis as a policy.

These, then, are some of the central features of the Jewish tradition which can serve as building blocks for a Jewish theology of liberation. Throughout history the Jewish people have been God's suffering servant, yet inspired by a vision of God's reign on earth they have been able to transcend their own misfortunes. In a post-Holocaust world, the message of human liberation has for Jewry been eclipsed by the commitment to Jewish survival. Christian liberation theology, however, with its focus on the desperate situation of those at the bottom of society, can act as a clarion call to the Jewish community, reminding them that Moses' plea to Pharaoh, 'let my people go', applies to all who desire freedom from oppression. The Jewish tradition points to God's Kingdom as the goal and hope of humanity: a world in which all peoples shall turn away from iniquity and injustice. This is not the hope of bliss in a future life, but the building up of the divine kingdom of truth and peace. Only by pursuing this goal can the Jewish people fulfil their divinely appointed task of being a light to all nations.

Bibliography

Araya, Victorio, 1987, *God of the Poor*, Maryknoll, New York: Orbis Books

Arendt, Hannah, 1951, *The Origins of Totalitarianism*, New York: Harcourt Brace

Ateek, Naim, 1989, *Justice and Only Justice: A Palestinian Theology of Liberation*, Maryknoll, New York: Orbis Books

Avineri, Shlomo, 1981, *The Making of Modern Zionism: The Intellectual Origins of the Jewish State*, New York: Basic Books

Bigo, Pierre, 1977, *The Church and Third World Revolution*, Maryknoll, New York: Orbis Books

Boff, Leonardo, 1978, *Jesus Christ Liberator*, Maryknoll, New York: Orbis Books

—— 1991 'Liberation Theology A Political Expression of Biblical Faith', in Otto Maduro (ed.), *Judaism, Christianity and Liberation: An Agenda For Dialogue*, Maryknoll, New York: Orbis Books

Brown, Robert M., 1978, *Theology in a New Key: Responding to Liberation Themes*, Philadelphia: Westminster

Camara, Dom Helder, 1976, *The Desert is Fertile*, New York: Jove Publications

Cohn-Sherbok, Dan, 1987, *On Earth as it is in Heaven: Jews, Christians and Liberation Theology*, Maryknoll, New York: Orbis Books

—— 1989, *Holocaust Theology*, London, Lamp Press

Cone, James, 1972, *The Spirituals and the Blues*, New York: Seabury

Cormie, Lee, 1981, 'The Challenge of Liberation Theology', in Richesin and Mahan (eds.), *The Challenge of Liberation Theology: A First World Response*, Maryknoll, New York: Orbis Books

—— 1981b, 'Liberation and Salvation', in Richesin and Mahan (eds.), *The Challenge of Liberation Theology: A First World Response*, Maryknoll, New York: Orbis Books

Croatto, J. Severino, 1981, *Exodus*, Maryknoll, New York: Orbis Books

Cussianovich, Alejandro, 1979, *Religious Life and the Poor: Liberation Theology Perspectives*, Dublin: Gill and MacMillan

Davies, J. G., 1976, *Christians, Politics and Violent Revolution*, Maryknoll, New York: Orbis Books

de Santa Ana, Julio, 1991, 'The Holocaust and Liberation', in Otto Maduro (ed.), *Judaism, Christianity and Liberation: An Agenda for Dialogue*, Maryknoll, New York: Orbis Books

Dussel, Enrique, 1976, *History and the Theology of Liberation*, Maryknoll, New York: Orbis Books

Echegoyen, M., 1971, 'Priests and Socialism in Chile', *New Blackfriars*, 52, 464ff.

Ellacuría, Ignacio, 1976, *Freedom Made Fresh*, Maryknoll, New York: Orbis Books

Ellis, Marc H. 1987, *Toward a Jewish Theology of Liberation*, Maryknoll, New York: Orbis Books

―――― 1989, *Toward a Jewish Theology of Liberation: The Uprising and the Future*, Maryknoll, New York: Orbis Books

―――― 1990, *Beyond Innocence and Redemption: Confronting the Holocaust and Israeli Power*, San Francisco: Harper and Row

Fackenheim, Emil, 1970, *God's Presence in History: Jewish Affirmations and Philosophical Reflections*, New York: New York University Press

―――― 1982, *To Mend the World: Foundations of Future Jewish Thought*, New York: Schocken Books

Feuerlicht, Roberta Strauss, 1983, *The Fate of the Jews: A People Torn Between Israeli Power and Jewish Ethics*, New York: Times Books

Fierro, Alfredo, 1977, *The Militant Gospel*, Maryknoll, New York: Orbis Books

Fleischer, Eva (ed.), 1977, *Auschwitz: Beginning of a New Era?*, New York: KTAV.

Gaon, Saadya, 1946, *The Book of Doctrines and Beliefs*

Gibellini, Rosino (ed.), 1980, *Frontiers of Theology in Latin America*, London: SCM Press

Greenberg, Irving, 1977, 'Cloud of Smoke, Pillar of Fire: Judaism, Christianity and Modernity After the Holocaust' in *Auschwitz: Beginning of a New Era?* ed. Eva Fleischner, New York: KTAV

Gutiérrez, Gustavo, 1973, *A Theology of Liberation*, Maryknoll, New York: Orbis Books

―――― 1983, *The Power of the Poor in History*, Maryknoll, New York: Orbis Books

Ha-Am, Ahad, 1946, *Essays, Letters and Memoirs*, ed. L. Simon, Oxford

Halevi, Judah, 1964, *The Kuzari*, New York: Schocken Books

Handy, Charles, 1983, 'The Future of Work', *Christian*, 8, 24–5

Hertzberg, Arthur, 1959, *The Zionist Idea*, New York: Athenaeum

Heschel, Abraham, 1969–71, *The Prophets*, New York: Harper and Row

Hillesum, Etty, 1985, *An Interrupted Life: The Diaries of Etty Hillesum, 1941–3*, London: Jonathan Cape, New York: Pocket Books

Jacobs, Louis, 1964, *Principles of the Jewish Faith*, London: Vallentine Mitchell

Joseph, Morris, 1903, *Judaism as Life and Creed*, London: Macmillan

Klenicki, Leon, 1988, *Christian-Jewish Relations*, 21.1

Kohler, Kaufman, 1916, 1968, *Jewish Theology*, New York: KTAV

Lazarus, Moritz, 1900, *The Ethics of Judaism*, Philadelphia: Jewish Publication Society

Lerner, Michael, 1991, 'Breaking the Chains of Necessity', and 'An Approach to Jewish Liberation Theology', in Otto Maduro (ed.), *Judaism, Christianity and Liberation: An Agenda for Dialogue*, Maryknoll, New York: Orbis Books

Levingston, Judd Kruger, 1991, 'Liberation Theology and Judaism', in Otto Maduro (ed.), *Judaism, Christianity and Liberation: An Agenda for Dialogue*, Maryknoll, New York: Orbis Books

Maduro, Otto (ed.), 1991, *Judaism, Christianity and Liberation: An Agenda for Dialogue*, Maryknoll, New York: Orbis Books

Míguez Bonino, José, 1965, *Doing Theology in a Revolutionary Situation*, Philadelphia: Fortress

Miranda, José P., 1974, *Marx and the Bible*, Maryknoll, New York: Orbis Books

Pérez-Esclarín, Antonio, 1978, *Atheism and Liberation*, Maryknoll, New York: Orbis Books

Perlmutter, Nathan & Ruth Ann, 1982, *The Real Anti Semitism in America*, New York: Arbor House

Reuther, Rosemary Radford, 1983, *Sexism and God-Talk*, Boston: Beacon Press

—— 1991, 'False Messianism and Prophetic Consciousness: Toward a Liberation Theology of Jewish-Christian Solidarity'

Richard, Pablo, 1991, 'Jewish and Christian Liberation Theology', in Otto Maduro (ed.), *Judaism, Christianity and*

Liberation: An Agenda for Dialogue, Maryknoll, New York: Orbis Books

Richesin, L. Dale and Mahan, Brian (eds.), 1981, *The Challenge of Liberation Theology: A First World Response*, Maryknoll, New York: Orbis Books

Rosenzweig, Franz, 'The Star of Redemption', in N. Glatzer, 1953, *Franz Rosenzweig: His Life and Thought*, New York

Rubenstein, Richard, 1991, 'Jews, Israel and Liberation Theology', in Otto Maduro (ed.), *Judaism, Christianity and Liberation: An Agenda for Dialogue*, Maryknoll, New York: Orbis Books 1966, After Auschwitz, Indiana: Bobbs-Merril, Maryknoll, New York: Orbis Books

Schechter, Solomon, 1961, *Aspects of Rabbinic Theology: Major Concepts of the Talmud*, New York: Schocken Books

Schneider, Susan, 1984, *Jewish and Female*, New York: Simon and Schuster

Shorris, Earl, 1982, *Jews without Mercy: A Lament*, New York: Doubleday

Sobrino, Jon, 1978, *Christology at the Crossroads: A Latin American Approach*, Maryknoll, New York: Orbis Books

Sölle, Dorothee, 1991, 'God's Pain and Our Pain: How Theology has to Change after Auschwitz', in Otto Maduro (ed.), *Judaism, Christianity and Liberation: An Agenda for Dialogue*, Maryknoll, New York: Orbis Books

Solomon, Norman, 1991, 'Economics and Liberation: Can the Theology of Liberation Decide Economic Questions?', in Otto Maduro (ed.), *Judaism, Christianity and Liberation, An Agenda for Dialogue*, Maryknoll, New York: Orbis Books

Spektor, I., 'Nachal Yitzchak', in S. Spero, *Morality, Halakha and the Jewish Tradition*, 134

Spero, S., 1983, *Morality, Halakha and the Jewish Tradition*, New York: KTAV

Tamez, Elsa, 1982, *Bible of the Oppressed*, Maryknoll, New York

Vincent, John, 1982, *Into the City*, London: Epworth Press

Wiesel, Elie, 1969, *Night*, New York: Avon

—— 1977, *The Trial of God*, New York: Random House

Rabbinic Sources

Agadoth Shir Hashirim: Rabbinic Commentary on the Song of Songs.

Avot (Sayings of the Fathers): Tractate in the Mishnah.

Avot de-Rabbi Nathan (Ab R.N.): Extra-canonical minor tractate of the Talmud.

Baba Batra (Bab B.): Tractate of the Talmud.

Baba Kamma: Tractate of the Talmud.

Baba Metzia: Tractate of the Talmud.

Deuteronomy Rabbah (Deut. R.): Rabbinic Commentary on the Book of Deuteronomy.

Exodus Rabbah (Ex. R.): (Midrash Shemot Rabbah): Rabbinic Commentary on the Book of Exodus.

Megillah: Tractate of the Talmud.

Midrash Psalms (Midr. Ps.): Rabbinic Commentary on the Book of Psalms.

Pe'ah: Tractate of the Talmud.

Pesahim: Tractate of the Talmud.

Pirke de Rabbi Eliezer: Rabbinic Commentary on Genesis and Exodus.

Shabbat (Shabb) (Sab.): Tractate of the Talmud.

Shevuot (Shebu'ot): Tractate of the Talmud.

Sifra: Rabbinic Commentary on Leviticus.

Sifre: Rabbinic Commentary on Numbers and Deuteronomy.

Sukkah (Suk.): Tractate of the Talmud.

Tanhuma (Tanh.) Rabbinic Commentary on the Torah.

Zohar: Medieval mystical work